TAB 1397

$10.95

WHAT TO DO WHEN
YOU GET YOUR HANDS ON A
MICROCOMPUTER

BY CHARLES P. HOLTZMAN

WHAT TO DO WHEN
YOU GET YOUR HANDS ON A
MICROCOMPUTER

To Mom

WHAT TO DO WHEN YOU GET YOUR HANDS ON A MICROCOMPUTER

BY CHARLES P. HOLTZMAN

TAB BOOKS Inc.
BLUE RIDGE SUMMIT, PA. 17214

FIRST EDITION

SECOND PRINTING

Copyright © 1982 by TAB BOOKS Inc.

Printed in the United States of America

Library of Congress Cataloging in Publication Data

Holtzman, Charles P.
    What to do when you get your hands on a microcomputer.

    Includes index.
    1. Microcomputers. I. Title.
QA76.5.H64   001.64'04   81-18219
ISBN 0-8306-0082-5   AACR2
ISBN 0-8306-1397-8 (pbk.)

Contents

2183781

Introduction

The day is April 30, 1983. An average American wakes up to the smell of hot coffee. He sits up and takes the cup from a little night stand and sips it quietly. His name is Mac and he talks in a quiet voice. "How was security last night, Dan?"

Dan, the home computer who communicates through a small speaker in the ceiling of the bedroom, answers in an equally calm, male voice. "As usual, nothing here. Noticed a breakin at Camarillo Heights about three AM. Their machine had the police there in three and one half minutes. Older person, of course."

Mac grunted. "They really should retrain themselves." There was quiet for a while as Mac sipped his coffee. He was always glad he had chosen Dan's voice. Some people had cheerful, bouncy voices in their machines. Mac hated cheerful, bouncy voices in the morning. Mac said, "The coffee is a tad warm."

"It will be a degree cooler in the morning."

Mac put his feet on the floor beside the bed. A tiny noise told him hot water, the exact amount and temperature for a shower, would be ready in two minutes. "Did you get hold of Mom?"

"She got home a little late and mentioned she was a little tired so I arranged for you to talk to her over breakfast. The weather is nice back in Indiana."

Dan knew not to call Mom early if the weather was not nice and that pleased Mac. He put his cup on the night stand and watched the refill quietly. "How is the world today?"

Dan's voice became even more calm and relaxed. "No big news on the wire services this morning. There is still trouble between Lebanon and Syria. Normal. Another coup in Salvador, bloodless. Russia and Japan signed a fishing treaty. The dollar and gold are unchanged on foreign exchanges." Dan paused, as he usually did, in case Mac wanted to comment. Mac sipped his coffee so Dan went on. "On the national scene, more riots in Florida. Crime statistics nationwide have dropped again. Particularly, of course, home burglaries. There is talk in Washington of a subway system for Los Angeles. The Army reports they need more volunteers. Two bills passed the Senate this morning, but I found them both boring." Dan paused again before going on to the local news. "There is some flooding damage still on Ventura Boulevard from the rains, but I've given the car an ideal bypass. I'll have a new route for you to drive to work by Friday anyway. It uses .03 less gas and is .02 safer to drive. One boat sank in the Ventura harbor. No lives lost. There was an assault in Oxnard at two AM, two burglaries in Port Hueneme, both stores at three AM, and a two car collision at four AM on 101 at the Seaward offramp. No deaths in any of the crimes or accidents."

Mac warmed his coffee again. "How about the home front?"

Dan chuckled. "Had a long chat with the new machine at the bank last night. Name is Lily. She finally admitted the eight dollar billing error and credited your account. I also talked to Fred, the one at the book club and told him to stop sending the book/tapes we never ordered. He tried to argue, but I solved that. Three unsolicited calls came in last night when you had me on hold. I got rid of the two salesmen. One of them even had a fake English accent. The third was your travel agent about your vacation."

Mac groaned. "Eleanor and I can't decide between Germany and Ireland." Dan chuckled sympathetically. "When I asked other machines, they recommended a quick tour of Germany with an extended rest in Ireland where the prices are much better." Mac answered, "Do it." Dan made a tiny humming noise for thirty seconds, then reported. "All room reservations, car rentals, airline tickets, and limo service from the house to the airport confirmed." Mac started for the shower and Dan spoke as Mac walked. "I have arranged for your right rear tire to be replaced at noon today. It is worn four hours too long. Your new car will be delivered in eighty-two days. I will arrange to have the new tire transferred to the new car as a spare."

Mac paused. "Any family business?"

"Shawn is due at the dentist at two PM, and Eleanor will be at a meeting, so I arranged with your office for you to take him. Your time has already been logged in and out with Oscar, your bookkeeper."

Mac frowned. "Is Oscar human?"

"No, just one of us. You have gained two ounces of weight since yesterday. I will balance that with a breakfast of half a grapefruit, two slices of toast, one egg, three strips of lean bacon, and decaffeinated coffee. After your shower, your clothes will be laid out, and your mother will be on screen one in the kitchen for a talk. Screen two will be *Casablanca*, part one. You will see part two on Saturday afternoon between playing golf at Montolvo and watching the new Broadway musical here. The rest of your schedule for the week is on your screen at work. Oh, I almost forgot. Today is your brother Frank's birthday. What is that one sincere line you wanted in his birthday letter?"

"Just put in something about my enjoying reading his latest mystery novel."

"No problem. I did read it. Fun book."

As he stepped into the automatic shower, Mac recalled with a small smile how complicated life used to be.

Nothing in this scenario is beyond present day technology. In other words, nothing new would have to be *discovered* for all of this to be possible.

In the world of computers new inventions come much more quickly than people can apply them. Most of this problem is with the *software*.

Software is a fancy word that means the list of instructions that a computer is supposed to follow. This list is also called a program. These programs are necessary because a computer is no smarter than a light bulb. The bulb doesn't know to turn on until you flip a switch. With enough lights and switches the effect can still be pretty spectacular. Think about the lighting at the last rock concert or opera (depending on your preference) that you saw. You *heard* the music, but you *saw* the show. During the weeks of rehearsal, the light operator spent hundreds of hours writing down on the script which lights to turn on and when. Yet the light itself is very simple.

Computers are similar. It is pretty easy to get a computer to add two numbers, or show you something, but to give it the exact instructions, in the exact order, to play Star Trek takes lots of time. Getting the computer to do all of the things described in the scenario would take even more time, but it can be done.

The major difference is that most computers don't have switches, they have a keyboard. You tell it what to do by typing in instructions. But how? What language do I use? You find yourself in the same dilemma as the traveler who is in a country where no one speaks the language he does. You may have enough money to hire all the servants in the country, but if you can't tell them what to do in a language they understand, it doesn't do any good to hire them. In fact, you probably *couldn't* hire them.

Communicating with the computer is what this book is all about. Most microcomputers do this in a language called BASIC. There are many other languages that computers can be taught to understand, but BASIC is the easiest one for humans to understand. The whole idea of computers is to make things easier for humans, so this is the language most microcomputer owners have chosen to include with their computer.

BASIC stands for Beginner's All-purpose Symbolic Instruction Code. The words in BASIC are code symbols that the BASIC interpreter can decode into instructions telling it what to do. To keep it simple enough for a beginner, the language is very general. It allows you to manipulate text as well as numbers, so it is an all-purpose language. Each of the words is like a magic power that unlocks the door to communicate with your computer.

As you progress through this book, you will learn 23 powers to control any computer using the BASIC language.

The powers are divided into four groups. The first group is the minimum vocabulary necessary to run a useful program. The second group adds some commands you can give the computer when it is not running a program, as well as introducing you to the computer's method of telling you when something is wrong. The third group contains the math, formatting, and instruction sequence words, as well as the method for giving the computer information while a program is running. This is the core of any programming language. The last group includes some special words that are used together to increase greatly the speed and power of the BASIC language. After each power small examples of how to use the power are shown. If you are lucky enough to have a computer, type in these examples to see how they work.

At the end of the groups are programs to show how the powers work together.

 **WARNING!**

Overload is a common problem for anyone working with a computer. A computer uses rigid logic. The human mind cannot always understand and adjust to this rigid logic. Sometimes the human mind becomes tired of the effort. That is overload. The cure is time away from computers.

Burnout is what happens when you spend too much time in overload. Overload is natural and temporary. BURNOUT is manic and permanent. BE CAREFUL!

Chapter 1

Say "Hi" to Your Computer

CRT—OR "THE BOOB TUBE"

The screen of a computer is sometimes called a crt, which stands for cathode ray tube. It is the same as the tube on a television set. Some computers come with a crt built in, some require you to hook up to a television set that you already own. You may want to save money by buying the kind that hooks to your own television, the quality of the picture is usually better if the computer comes with its own. A color computer will have to be hooked up to a color television or monitor (a crt made just for computers) to use the color features. A black and white television or monitor will work with most color computers, but you will not be able to use the color features properly.

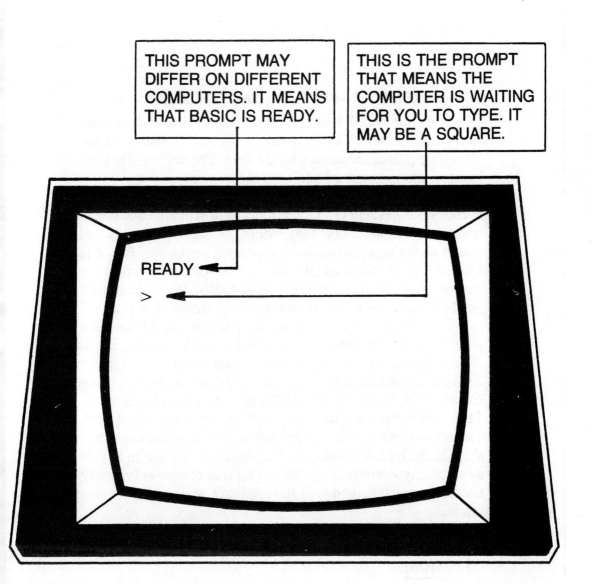

THIS PROMPT MAY DIFFER ON DIFFERENT COMPUTERS. IT MEANS THAT BASIC IS READY.

THIS IS THE PROMPT THAT MEANS THE COMPUTER IS WAITING FOR YOU TO TYPE. IT MAY BE A SQUARE.

READY

>

KEYBOARD—OR "THE SILENT TYPEWRITER"

Each keyboard looks similar to a typewriter, but no keyboard is exactly like a typewriter. Also, keyboards on different computers are never exactly alike. The keyboard is what humans use to communicate with the computer.

Messages are typed one character at a time. The computer decodes the key, checks to see if it is a key that means something specific, and if not, remembers the value of the key and puts it on the screen. Because a computer works very fast, this takes very little time, and it looks like the character appears at the same instant you type the key. It doesn't matter how slow you type. Computers are patient and will wait for slow humans.

Once your message is typed in, you may expect the computer to read it immediately, and if it is an order, to execute it. Wrong. How does the computer know that you are done typing? Every keyboard has a key that we call the action key. On some computers it is labeled RETURN, on others it is labeled ENTER. Some may even have EOF which stands for end of field. The action key is usually on the right hand side of the keyboard, about in the middle, similar to the position of the return key on an electric typewriter. Find that key on your computer (you may need the manual to help you) and use it at any time you see this symbol.

ACTION

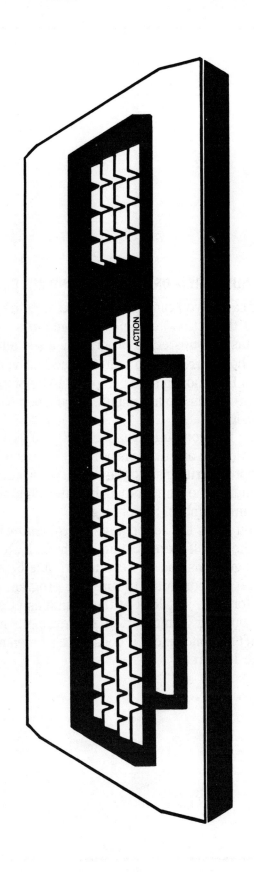

5

LINE NUMBERS—OR "ADDRESS AND ZIP CODE"

In most cases, you can type a BASIC statement into your computer, hit the action key, and the computer will instantly perform the task requested. A program is a sequence of these instructions, however, and no matter how fast you type, you could not do it fast enough for a computer to be of much help in solving long problems. Your computer would be no more than a fancy calculator.

To make the computer realize that you are entering a series of instructions and that it is not to perform until you tell it to (in other words, writing a program), you put a number in front of each statement. The number must be different for each line. It is called the line number. Simple right?

When you press the action key, the computer looks at the beginning of the line. If there is a number there, it stores the line as part of a program instead of executing it immediately. We will see how to get the computer to run your program in the next chapter, but for now, just look at the examples closely before trying them on your computer. If the example has no line numbers, don't use one, and if it does have a line number make sure you type it correctly.

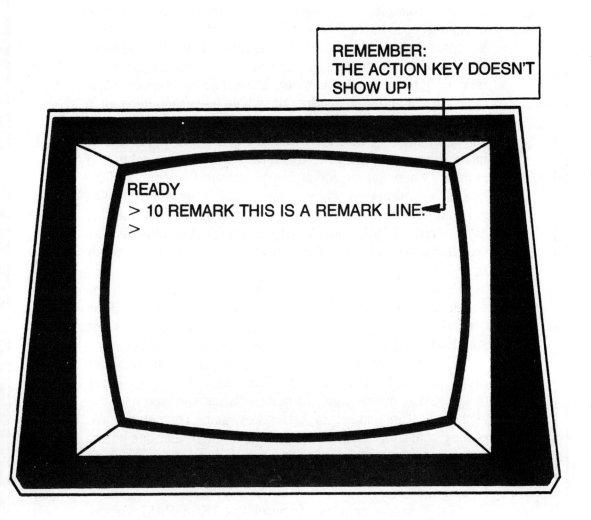

MEMORY—OR "LIKE THE ELEPHANT, I NEVER FORGET."

Another part of your computer that makes it more than just a fancy calculator is the memory. There are many different kinds of memory, but all microcomputers have one kind in common. It is called random access memory (RAM). RAM is used for many different things in the computer, but regardless of what it is used for, it is physically the same as any other section of RAM.

For example, when you are typing in a message to your computer, each letter is stored in an area of memory called the keyboard buffer. When you hit the action key, the computer looks at the line in the keyboard buffer and checks for a line number. If there is a line number, it is not going to execute this message right now, so it stores the whole line in another spot in memory called the BASIC text area. There are also special places in memory that the computer sets aside to remember intermediate answers (like the total from the first column of numbers when you are adding two columns), the number of the line it is working on when it is running your program, and anything else it needs to keep track of. There is nothing that says an area of RAM must be used for a specific purpose. The area that stores a line of BASIC text now could store a number later.

When you are working with your computer in BASIC, you do not have to worry about what memory is used for what. The computer keeps track of that. You only need to make sure that you don't write a program so big that you run out of memory.

Memory size is measured in bytes, and most computer people refer to 1024 bytes as a K. Each byte will store one letter of a sentence, or one digit of a number when you type it on the keyboard. After you hit the action key, some computers have codes that allow them to make a byte store more than one letter, or two bytes to store more than a two-digit number. You don't need to worry about that. On your screen it all comes out looking the same.

The smallest popular computer has 1K of RAM and the largest ones have 64K. As you learn BASIC you will write longer programs, but you will also learn ways to find out how much memory you are using. For right now, all of the programs in this book can be run on a 1K computer.
Let's get to it!

Chapter 2

Group 1

The four powers of communication in this section will enable you to run a real program. The concepts they use are at the foundation of everything you will ever do with computers. Group 1 includes the words LET, PRINT, END, and RUN. These are common English words, and their meaning in BASIC is nearly identical to English usage.

LET—OR "THE MAGIC WAND"

LET is like a magician's wand that makes things appear in an empty box, or a box that had something else in it at first. The boxes have labels that you assign. The boxes are roughly equivalent to memory locations. The computer remembers the location, what you labeled it, and what you put it in. You only have to remember the label to find out what the contents are. For example, if you say LET A=10 $\boxed{\text{ACTION}}$ the computer will label a section of memory with the A, will store 10 there, and then either go on to the next program instruction or wait for you to type in something else. There is no indication on the screen that the computer has done anything, because you didn't tell the computer to do anything else—just store the number.

The number can also be an arithmetic statement. LET B=2+5 $\boxed{\text{ACTION}}$ is perfectly acceptable. B would have the value 7 stored in it. LET C=A−B $\boxed{\text{ACTION}}$ would store the number 3 in C.

REMEMBER THAT THE
ACTION KEY IS
PRESSED AT THE END
OF EACH LINE. IT
DOESN'T SHOW ON THE SCREEN.

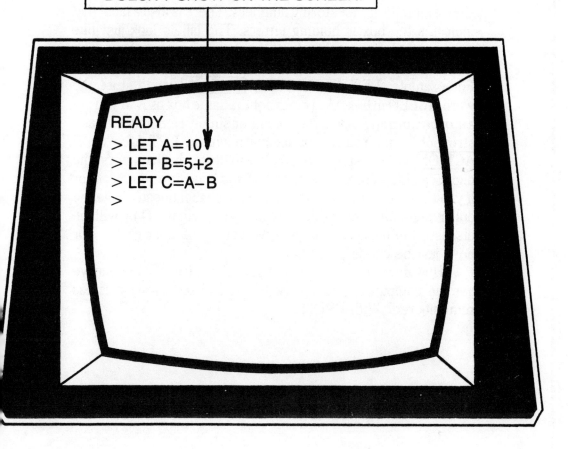

READY
> LET A=10
> LET B=5+2
> LET C=A−B
>

There are two different kinds of labels in BASIC. The kind shown already are for storing numbers. There is also a label that indicates the box is holding letters. The labels look just like number labels except that there is a dollar sign after them. The letters you want put in the box must have quotes around them. For example, LET A$="HELLO" ACTION would store the word HELLO in box A$. This is not the same box as A. If you put a *number* into an A$ box, the computer simply remembers it as a string of digits. You cannot use math with it. LET A$="5+2" ACTION will not store 7 in A$. It will store, as characters, the digit 5, a plus sign, and the digit 2. If you leave the quotes off, or if you try to use quotes with a box whose label doesn't have the dollar sign, the computer will not work right. This will be discussed in more detail when we get to the next group. For now, just be careful.

How do we really know that box A has 10 in it? How can we get the computer to talk back to us, and tell us what it has remembered? With PRINT.

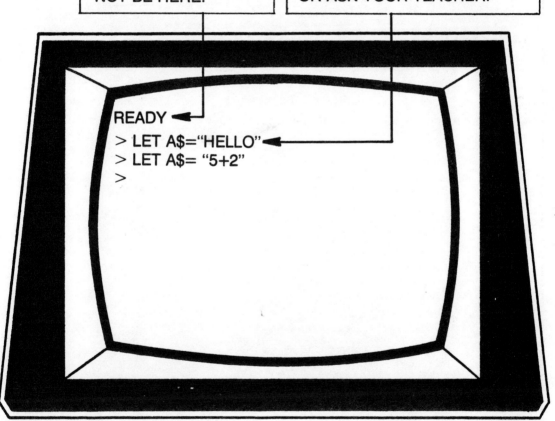

UNLESS YOU HAVE SHUT THE COMPUTER OFF SINCE THE LAST EXAMPLE, THE READY PROMPT WILL NOT BE HERE.

IF YOUR COMPUTER DOESN'T HAVE THE DOUBLE QUOTE ON IT, USE THE SINGLE QUOTE. IF THAT DOESN'T WORK, LOOK IN THE MANUAL OR ASK YOUR TEACHER.

```
READY
> LET A$="HELLO"
> LET A$= "5+2"
>
```

Print

PRINT—OR "SHOW ME"

A computer would have no value at all unless it could tell you the answers to the problems it has solved. The PRINT statement is what is used most of the time to achieve this. Rarely will you write a program without a PRINT statement in it, but the kinds of information you want to PRINT will vary so this statement has several forms.

The first form is called the string literal or literal string. Anything that you put in quotes after a PRINT will be literally printed in the screen. The examples (as you have probably figured out) are on the screen in the illustration to the right. The PRINT statement is dumb though. You can put anything inside the quotes and, no matter how ridiculous, the computer will faithfully print it. If you are following along on a computer, your screen should look like the one to the right.

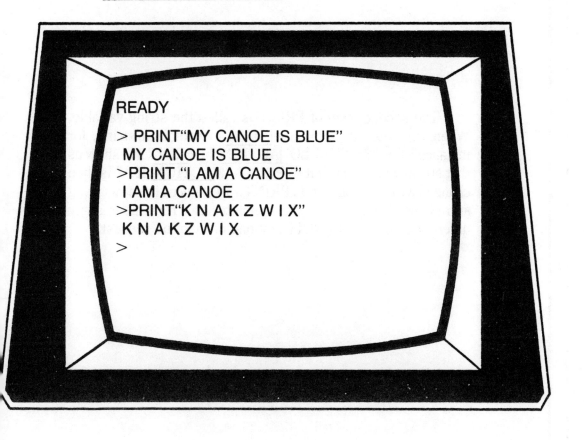

DON'T FORGET THE
ACTION KEY!

READY

> PRINT"MY CANOE IS BLUE"
 MY CANOE IS BLUE
>PRINT "I AM A CANOE"
 I AM A CANOE
>PRINT"K N A K Z W I X"
 K N A K Z W I X
>

The second form of PRINT is called the string variable. When we cause the box labeled A$ to contain a string, for instance LET A$= "HELLO" ACTION the PRINT will show us that string when we tell it to PRINT A$ ACTION . If A$ is then changed with a second LET, PRINT will show us the new string stored there. Of course, the computer can remember many different strings and PRINT any one of them on request.

IF YOU GET TO THE
BOTTOM OF THE SCREEN,
DON'T WORRY! THE
TOP LINE WILL
DISAPPEAR AND ALL
OF THE OTHERS WILL
MOVE UP TO MAKE ROOM.
THIS IS CALLED SCROLLING

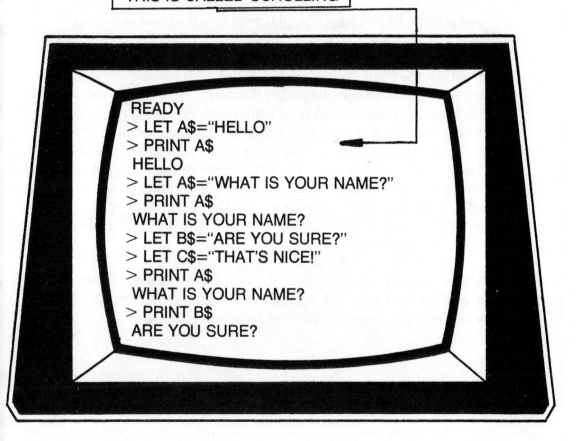

```
READY
> LET A$="HELLO"
> PRINT A$
 HELLO
> LET A$="WHAT IS YOUR NAME?"
> PRINT A$
 WHAT IS YOUR NAME?
> LET B$="ARE YOU SURE?"
> LET C$="THAT'S NICE!"
> PRINT A$
 WHAT IS YOUR NAME?
> PRINT B$
 ARE YOU SURE?
```

The next form of PRINT is the numeric variable. This lets you print the value stored in boxes with numeric names. For instance, if you said LET A=10 ACTION , and then told the computer to PRINT A ACTION ,it would put the value in box A, which is 10, on the screen.

Just as the LET will allow you to add two numeric variables together, the PRINT will allow you to print two variables added together. The example illustrates this point. You can also subtract, multiply, divide, and raise numbers to a certain power. If you haven't learned about decimal places and exponents, don't worry, you don't have to use them to work on a computer. When you are ready to use them, they will be there waiting. Also, if the computer you are using only has integer BASIC (which means it only deals with whole numbers) the divide will only return whole numbers, so the example PRINT A/B ACTION would print 3 on the screen.

A numeric variable can be used more than once in a PRINT statement, and you don't have to stop at two variables. The example uses three, and the limit depends on what computer you are using. Most will allow at least one line full!

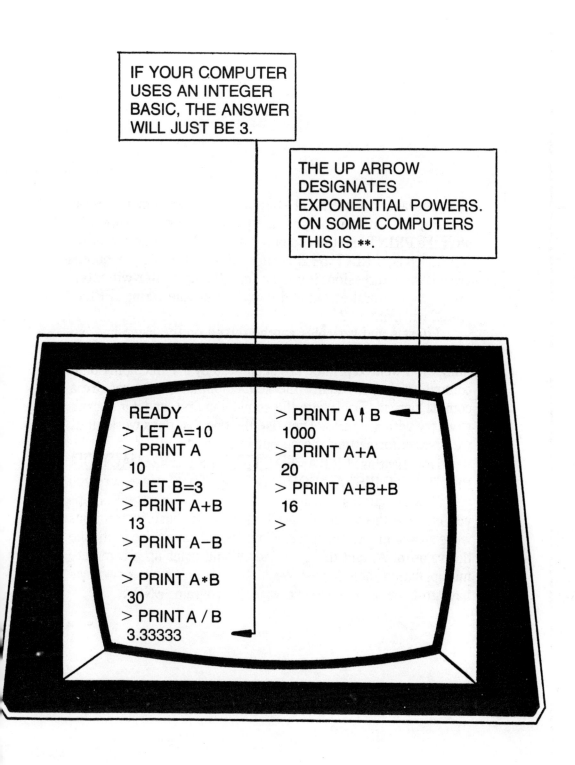

IF YOUR COMPUTER USES AN INTEGER BASIC, THE ANSWER WILL JUST BE 3.

THE UP ARROW DESIGNATES EXPONENTIAL POWERS. ON SOME COMPUTERS THIS IS **.

```
READY                > PRINT A ↑ B
> LET A=10           1000
> PRINT A            > PRINT A+A
10                   20
> LET B=3            > PRINT A+B+B
> PRINT A+B          16
13                   >
> PRINT A−B
7
> PRINT A*B
30
> PRINT A / B
3.33333
```

The last form of PRINT statement is called numeric literal. As in the LET statement, you can type an arithmetic expression after the PRINT and the computer will evaluate it before printing it. Thus, PRINT 5+2 would yield 7. Do not put quotes around the expression. If you do that, the computer will interpret it as a literal string and simply print the string. PRINT "5+2" will print 5+2.

Literals and variables can be mixed on the same line, so PRINT "5+2=";5+2 will print out 5+2=7. Notice that the two things you wanted printed are separated by a semicolon. Some computers do not require the semicolon, and some require a comma instead. Try it with the semicolon first, and if it doesn't work try with a comma. Then use the one that does work, until we discuss formatting the output in more detail.

Now try this. LET A=5 ACTION. LET B=2*A ACTION. PRINT "2 TIMES";A; "EQUALS ";B ACTION. Make sure you get all of the quotes and semicolons placed correctly. Perhaps you can see the value of variables now. If these instructions were stored in the computer, all we would have to do is change the value of A, and the computer would print up a complete multiplication table for us! Well, there is one more power we have to know before we can write a program. END.

THERE ARE FOUR
QUOTES AND THREE
SEMICOLONS IN THIS
LINE. MAKE SURE
YOU GET ALL OF
THEM.

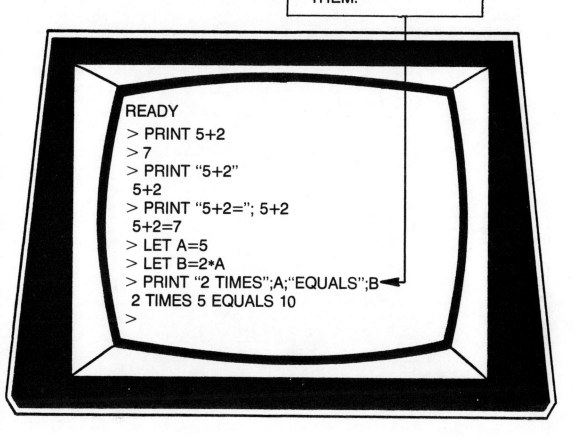

```
READY
> PRINT 5+2
> 7
> PRINT "5+2"
 5+2
> PRINT "5+2="; 5+2
 5+2=7
> LET A=5
> LET B=2*A
> PRINT "2 TIMES";A;"EQUALS";B
 2 TIMES 5 EQUALS 10
>
```

END—or "STOP!"

The END power does exactly what it says. Some computers demand that at least one END be in the program. Some demand that there be an END after the last instruction the computer is supposed to do *even though it is obvious that there are no more instructions*! On some computers the END is called STOP, which is just as obvious. You may find, when you run your first programs, that your computer knows what both words mean, and just ends the program, while the other stops the program and tells you what line you stopped on. If this happens, use the one that just ends the program until later in this book.

In future programs there will be times when the END is absolutely necessary. For the programs we are doing right now it may be unnecessary on your computer. Use it anyway for two reasons. One, it is good programming practice. Two, there will be no doubt about whether your computer needs it or not.

The END statement is only used in programs, so there is no need to type it in without a line number. So, let's type it in *with* a line number, along with a few other statements and make a program. Type in the program in the illustration, and see if your screen looks like ours.

There it sits. Your first program! You have probably noted that the computer hasn't done anything yet. Your program is on the screen, and it is stored inside the computer too. How do we make the computer do these things in the program? Read on.

AT THIS POINT IT
WOULD PROBABLY BE
A GOOD IDEA TO SHUT
OFF THE MACHINE AND
TURN IT BACK ON, OR
CLEAR THE SCREEN IF
YOU KNOW HOW. PROMPT
WILL APPEAR.

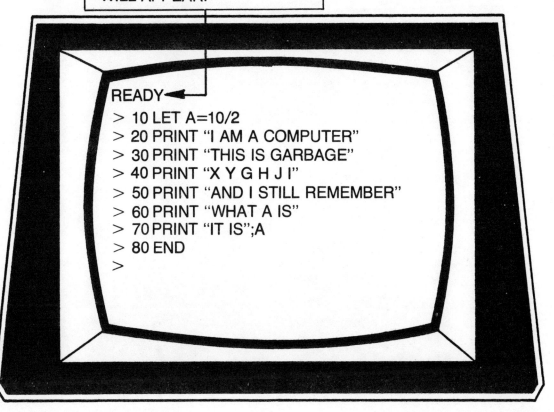

READY
> 10 LET A=10/2
> 20 PRINT "I AM A COMPUTER"
> 30 PRINT "THIS IS GARBAGE"
> 40 PRINT "X Y G H J I"
> 50 PRINT "AND I STILL REMEMBER"
> 60 PRINT "WHAT A IS"
> 70 PRINT "IT IS";A
> 80 END
>

RUN—OR "CARRY OUT MY ORDERS"

Before you do anything else, do this. Type in the last example. Now type in RUN ACTION. Viola!

The RUN power describes itself. It tells the computer to do whatever job has been ordered. When the computer sees this word, it searches through the BASIC text buffer and finds the lowest numbered line. It does whatever that line says to do, and then finds the next lowest line and does that. This continues until an END is found, at which time it stops.

The RUN power can be put into a numbered line. When the computer sees it, it will stop whatever it was doing and start the program all over again. Before you try this, make sure you know where the BREAK, or RESET, key is, or how to turn the computer off and back on.

Example: The program is still in your computer. Even if the whole program isn't on the screen, it is still in the BASIC text buffer. Type in 80 RUN ACTION. This erases the old line 80 and replaces it with a new one that says RUN. Now if you type RUN ACTION (no number this time) you will see the computer run your program over and over. If you turn off the computer and turn it back on, the program will be lost. If you use BREAK it will still be there. RESET varies from one computer to another, so I don't know if it will be there or not on your computer. We are done with this example anyway.

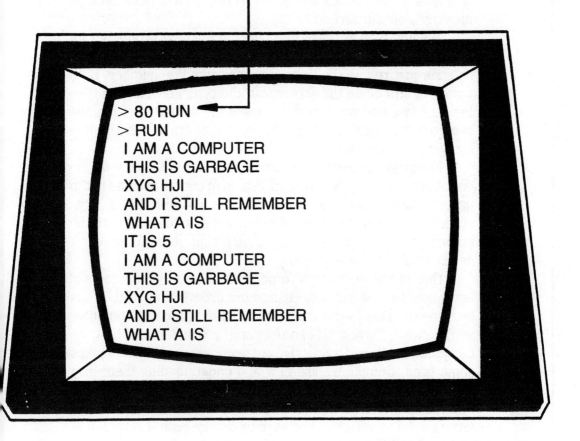

NOTICE THAT WHEN YOU
PUT A LINE NUMBER IN
FRONT OF RUN THE
COMPUTER STORES IT
INSTEAD OF DOING IT.

> 80 RUN
> RUN
I AM A COMPUTER
THIS IS GARBAGE
XYG HJI
AND I STILL REMEMBER
WHAT A IS
IT IS 5
I AM A COMPUTER
THIS IS GARBAGE
XYG HJI
AND I STILL REMEMBER
WHAT A IS

GROUP 1 SAMPLE PROGRAMS

Now, before you overload, you get to just play around with what you already know. Make sure you are certain what the action key does to a line, with or without a line number. Familiarize yourself with the keyboard.

If you have a keyboard with numbers at the top (like on a typewriter) *and* numbers at the side (like on a calculator) experiment and you will probably find that they work alike. If you have a computer that prints upper case letters (capitals) only, you might actually press shift while you are typing (particularly if you have used a typewriter before). You will see that the letter comes out the same on the screen, but the computer will not like it if it is in one of the command words. It will print strange messages on the screen.

We will look at these messages in the next group, but for now just retype the line and run the program again. To correct an error just retype the line using the same line number. Both lines will still be on the screen, but the computer only remembers the last one you typed. It erases the old one that had the same number. You will also find that you can erase an entire line by typing its number and just pressing the action key.

Probably the hardest thing to remember will be the difference between an arithmetic expression in quotes and one not in quotes. Remember that quotes always go with the $ sign, regardless of what is inside of them, and no quotes go with the numeric variables that don't have the $ sign. Reread the text if necessary.

One of the best ways to put orders into a computer and learn how they work is to change the orders after a RUN has been done. This helps you to understand how the computer works. Never leave a list of orders until you understand how the computer thinks and works. Do not become worried if this takes some time. Computers are new and understanding them may take a while. Change at least one line in each of the lists of orders in the examples you have just typed in. When you change letters used as variables, be sure to change both the LET line and the PRINT line to match up.

```
10 LET A=1
20 LET B=2
30 LET C=3
40 PRINT "THIS WILL TYPE EACH NUMBER ON A SEP-
   ARATE LINE"
50 PRINT A
60 PRINT B
70 PRINT C
80 PRINT "AND THESE ARE ON THE SAME LINE"
90 PRINT A;B;C
100 END
```

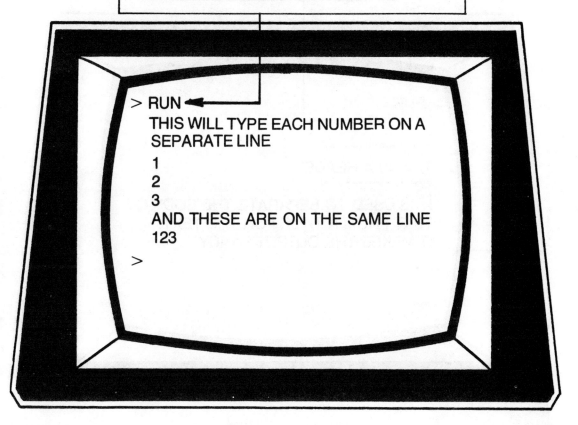

IF YOU DON'T KNOW HOW TO CLEAR
THE SCREEN, THIS RUN WILL COME
RIGHT AFTER THE PROGRAM LISTING.

DO WE HAVE TO REMIND YOU TO PRESS
THE ACTION KEY AFTER RUN?

> RUN

THIS WILL TYPE EACH NUMBER ON A
SEPARATE LINE
1
2
3
AND THESE ARE ON THE SAME LINE
123

>

```
 10 LET A$="*"
 20 LET B$="THIS IS A HEADER"
 30 PRINT
 40 PRINT
 50 PRINT
 60 PRINT A$; A$; A$; A$; A$; A$; A$; A$; A$; A$; A$; A$; A$; A$; A$; A$;
 70 PRINT B$
 80 PRINT A$; A$; A$; A$; A$; A$; A$; A$; A$; A$; A$; A$; A$; A$; A$; A$;
 90 PRINT "IT IS USED TO SEPARATE THE BODY OF
100 PRINT "TEXT FROM A TITLE FOR THE TEXT."
110 PRINT "IT MAKES THE OUTPUT FANCY."
120 END
```

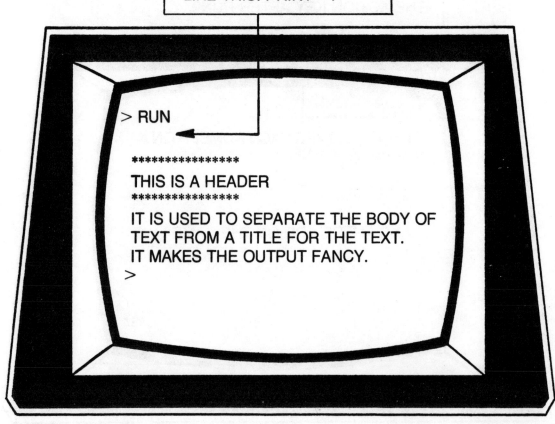

LINES 30-50 SAY TO
PRINT NOTHING, SO THE
COMPUTER DOES!
YOUR COMPUTER MAY
REQUIRE A BLANK
LIKE THIS: PRINT" ".

> RUN

****
THIS IS A HEADER
****
IT IS USED TO SEPARATE THE BODY OF
TEXT FROM A TITLE FOR THE TEXT.
IT MAKES THE OUTPUT FANCY.
>

```
 10 LET A=20
 20 LET B=10
 30 LET A$="A+B="
 40 LET B$="A-B="
 50 LET C$="A*B="
 60 LET D$="A/B="
 70 PRINT A$;A+B
 80 PRINT B$;A-B
 90 PRINT C$;A*B
100 PRINT D$;A/B
110 PRINT Z
1200 END
```

SINCE YOU DIDN'T TELL
THE COMPUTER WHAT Z
WAS EQUAL TO, THE
BOX (VARIABLE) STILL
CONTAINED ZERO, SO
THAT'S WHAT IT PRINTED!
YOUR COMPUTER MAY
PRINT A RANDOM
NUMBER INSTEAD.

NOTICE THAT ANY
LINE NUMBER LARGER
THAN THE LAST ONE
IS OK. AS LONG AS
IT DOESN'T EXCEED
THE HIGHEST NUMBER YOUR
MACHINE CAN DO.

EXPERIMENT:
CHANGE Z TO Z$ IN LINE 110.
ADD LINE 120 PRINT "****".
THEN RUN. WHAT DID THE
COMPUTER PRINT BETWEEN
A/B=2 AND ****? THAT IS
WHAT A STRING VARIABLE HAS
IN IT IF YOU DON'T ASSIGN
IT A VALUE WITH LET.

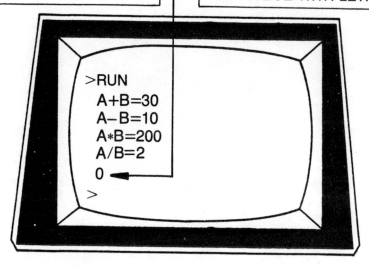

```
>RUN
 A+B=30
 A-B=10
 A*B=200
 A/B=2

 0

>
```

At this point stop and take a look around you. Has everybody else gone home? If you are at home, has everybody else gone to bed? How long have you been working with your new-found friend?

Beware of overload! If you are tired, or have other things to do, it is time to stop for a while. Many a programmer has ignored the warning signs and proceeded into the realms of BURNOUT. You have to learn when to get up and leave. It is as important as learning the language when working with computers.

When you come back, type in the last example from this group and go on to the next chapter.

Chapter 3

Group 2

While you were experimenting with the sample problems in group 1, you probably realized that there must be an easier way to keep track of what you were doing. With lines scrolling off the screen, and more than one version of a line on the screen at any given time, and even meaningless messages appearing from time to time, you might have decided that this computing business isn't all its cracked up to be. Well, history will decide if you are right about the second part of that statement, but you are certainly correct if you believe there are easier ways to edit programs.

The powers introduced in this group will enable you to quickly make and check any changes you care to make in a program. Some of these powers can be used in programs themselves. These will be noted.

CLS—OR "CLEAN UP THIS ACT"

The purpose of this power is to clear everything off the screen and put the prompt (called a cursor) in the upper left corner of the screen. This is also called the home position. For this reason, the command is called HOME on some computers.

This is one of those confusing commands that every company does differently, so it might also be called CLR, CLEAR, or CALL CLEAR on your computer. In addition, there are usually two ways of getting the computer to do this. You can either type in the word, in which case it is just like any other command, or, on most computers, you can press a single key marked with one of the words above that will also clear the screen. This is definitely a time to dig out the manual or ask your teacher.

There are two notes to add here. One, some computers do not have a clear screen function so to get all of the garbage off of it you simply press the action key enough times to scroll everything off. The problem is that the cursor does not return to the home position. Two, if you see the CLEAR command with a number after it, your computer has one of the other commands to clear the screen. CLEAR with a number means something else.

Once you have found the proper key or command, use it and see if your screen looks like the illustration. Remember, just because the program is erased from the screen doesn't mean it is gone. It is still stored in the BASIC text buffer. If you want to see it again, use the next power, LIST.

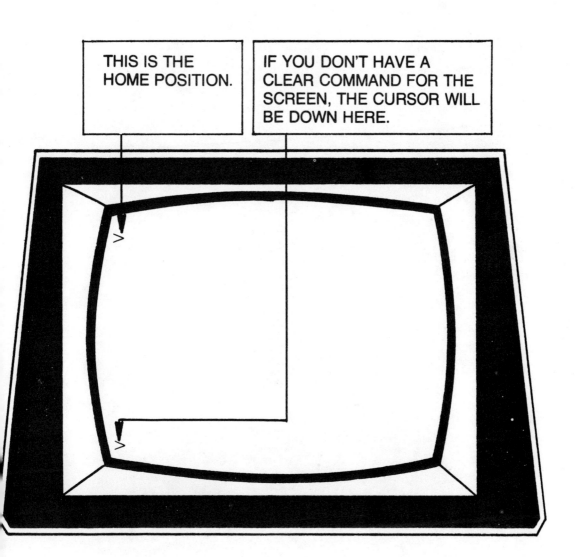

LIST—OR "LET ME COUNT THE LINES"

LIST puts your program back on the screen so you can see it, and make sure all of the lines are right, or that none of them are left out. It copies what is in the BASIC text buffer onto the screen. Your program is now in both places, just like when you first typed it in. Now try this with the example you have loaded. Type in a LET statement and give it line number 5. Then clear the screen and LIST ACTION again. Where did line 5 go?

You might have expected it to be the last line in the program, since it is the last line you typed, but BASIC rearranges them, puts them in order, LIST prints them on the screen in order. Nice, huh?

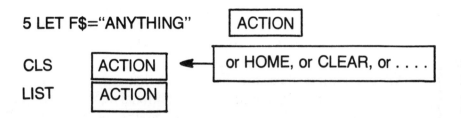

5 LET F$="ANYTHING"   ACTION

CLS   ACTION   ◄──   or HOME, or CLEAR, or . . . .

LIST   ACTION

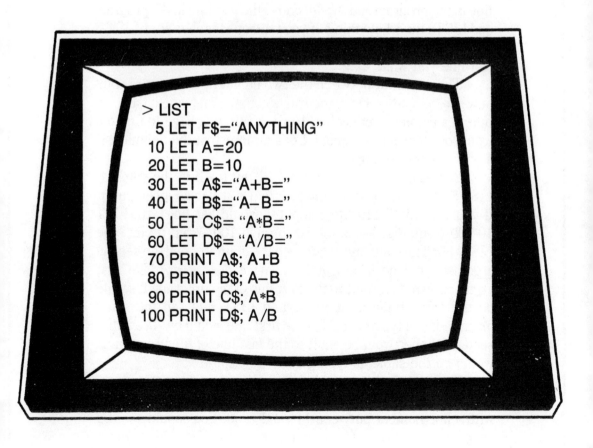

```
> LIST
  5 LET F$="ANYTHING"
 10 LET A=20
 20 LET B=10
 30 LET A$="A+B="
 40 LET B$="A−B="
 50 LET C$= "A*B="
 60 LET D$= "A/B="
 70 PRINT A$; A+B
 80 PRINT B$; A−B
 90 PRINT C$; A*B
100 PRINT D$; A/B
```

If the program you are listing has more lines in it than the screen can hold, you may find the line you want has scrolled off of the screen before you can read it. As you write longer programs, this can be a problem. Therefore, LIST has several options in most BASICS.

First, there are three words that must be defined. When a command is required to have additional information after it, that additional information is called an *argument*. Thus, in PRINT A$, A$ is the argument. If more than one argument is or can be used, the punctuation between them is called a *delimiter*. So PRINT A$;B$, has a semicolon as a delimiter. If the command is supposed to have an argument but the computer assumes a certain value automatically if you don't use an argument, that value is called a *default* value.

LIST requires two arguments on most computers. The first one tells what line number to start with, and the second tells what line number to end at. If you don't put any numbers after LIST, the computer assumes the first number is the first line in the program and the second is the last line in the program and LISTs the whole thing. If you type one number after LIST it just prints that line number. It assumes it is both the first and last line you want.

The delimiter between the two numbers varies from computer to computer. On some it is a comma, on some a dash, on others a colon or semicolon. Here, again, you have to find out from your teacher or manual. Let's assume that the delimiter is a dash for this example.

You already know that LIST all by itself is the same as LIST 5-1200 if the last sample program is still in your computer. If you said LIST 110 the computer would list line 110. LIST 10-100 would list just lines 10 through 100. What if you type LIST -80? The computer would see the delimiter and the second argument, but no first argument. What does it do? The first argument would default to the first line of the program. It would do the same thing as if you typed LIST 5-80. In the same manner, if you typed LIST 70- the first line would be 70, and the second number would default to the last line of the program. It would be the same as typing LIST 70-1200.

Once you find out the delimiters for your computer, practice with this for a while. Also, try inserting a LIST statement with a line number between 110 and 1200. You should see the program listed right after the program prints 0 on the screen.

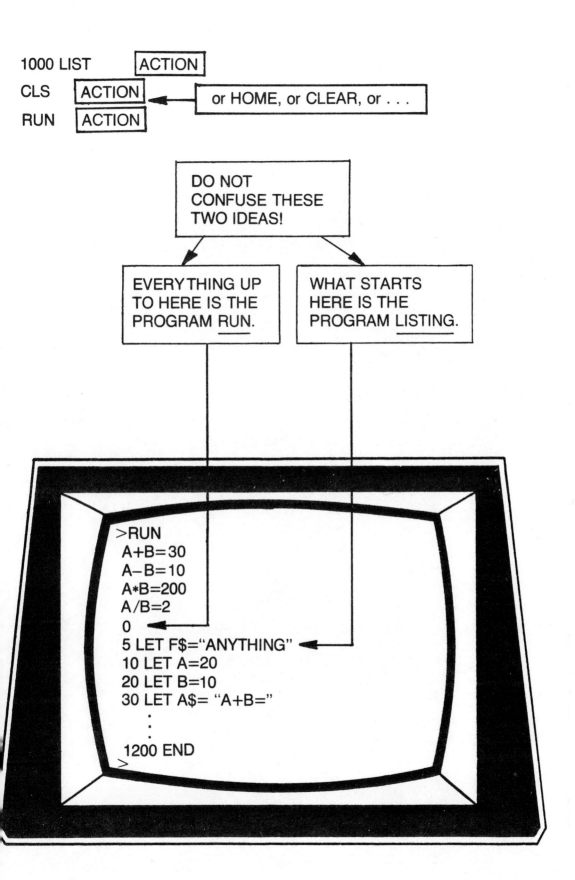

1000 LIST ACTION

CLS ACTION ◄─── or HOME, or CLEAR, or . . .

RUN ACTION

DO NOT
CONFUSE THESE
TWO IDEAS!

EVERYTHING UP
TO HERE IS THE
PROGRAM RUN.

WHAT STARTS
HERE IS THE
PROGRAM LISTING.

```
>RUN
A+B=30
A−B=10
A*B=200
A/B=2
0
5 LET F$="ANYTHING"
10 LET A=20
20 LET B=10
30 LET A$= "A+B="
     .
     .
     .
1200 END
>
```

DELETE—OR "CUT! CUT!"

DELETE does just what it says. It deletes lines from the program. The arguments for DELETE are almost the same as those for LIST. The only difference is that DELETE by itself, with no arguments, will not assume any default values. Instead it does nothing. This is for your protection, because once the line is deleted the only way to get it back is to retype it.

Generally if you want to DELETE just one line you must type in the line number and press the action key. But if you have a whole block of lines, or if you want to delete some lines in the middle of a program *that is still running*, you use DELETE.

For example, in the program we are still working with, line 5 has become useless. Let's say we also want to get rid of lines 10 and 20 but we don't yet know what we will replace them with. DELETE 5-20 would take care of this for us.

Remember when we discussed memory we talked about memory being used to hold the BASIC text *and* intermediate results, tables, and variables? Suppose you had a program so long that the number of bytes left was not sufficient to store all those results and variables. What you could do would be to place your opening instructions and introduction at the beginning of the program. When they were done running, the next instruction would delete those lines, leaving enough room for the variables that will be assigned later in the program. The figure to the right illustrates this. Remember that this is a very advanced procedure and should only be used when absolutely necessary. You may even find that your computer won't allow this, in which case you will only use DELETE as an editing tool outside of the program (which means without a line number in front of it).

```
  5 CLS
 10  PRINT "THIS PROGRAM DEMONSTRATES DELETE"
 20  PRINT "BEING USED TO GET RID OF THE INTRODUCTION"
 30  PRINT "TO MAKE MORE ROOM IN MEMORY"
 40  PRINT " NOW THAT YOU HAVE READ THIS"
 50  PRINT "IT WILL BE DELETED"
 60  PRINT "FROM THE PROGRAM, BUT NOT THE SCREEN"
 70  DELETE 5-70
 80  LET A=200
 90  PRINT A*123
100  END
```

TO ENTER THIS PROGRAM YOU MUST
FIRST DELETE THE OLD PROGRAM.
HOW DID YOU DELETE THE OLD
PROGRAM? DID YOU USE
DELETE 5-1200? THERE IS
AN EASIER WAY; THE POWER
NEW.

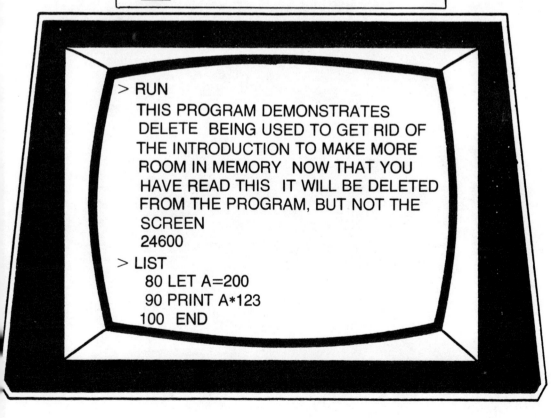

```
> RUN
  THIS PROGRAM DEMONSTRATES
  DELETE  BEING USED TO GET RID OF
  THE INTRODUCTION TO MAKE MORE
  ROOM IN MEMORY  NOW THAT YOU
  HAVE READ THIS  IT WILL BE DELETED
  FROM THE PROGRAM, BUT NOT THE
  SCREEN
  24600
> LIST
    80 LET A=200
    90 PRINT A*123
   100  END
```

NEW—OR "OOPS!"

As you recall, we said that DELETE was just like LIST except that DELETE had no power to assume default values for both variables. The reasoning here was that it would be too easy for an accident to occur, wiping out your entire program, while using DELETE. Instead, the power NEW is used for that purpose.

NEW has no arguments and wipes out all variables stored in memory when it wipes out the program. In a sense it wipes the memory clean in preparation for a new program. So, if you are going to use a computer that someone else was working at, the second thing you should do is to type NEW ACTION. Notice I said the *second* thing. The first thing you must do is to make certain the person who used it before you is finished!

You will learn about mass storage of programs later in this book, but now is a good time to mention that if you ever write a program that you think is good enough to sell, you will probably sell it on some form of mass media, like cassette or disk. One way to give yourself a small amount of protection against piracy (someone stealing your software) is to end your program with a NEW instead of, or just before, the END statement. This way, when the program is done running, it will erase itself from memory. A smart programmer can get around this every time, but it does offer one small "lock" on your software. Note: Always use an END statement while you are writing and correcting your program. Only change the END to NEW after the program is saved to cassette or disk, and you are ready to make your copies. Otherwise, you may lose many hours of work with one little accident.

LIST   ACTION

99 NEW   ACTION

LIST   ACTION

RUN   ACTION

LIST   ACTION

THE PROGRAM IS GONE!

NEW IS USUALLY USED
WITHOUT A LINE NUMBER
AND EXECUTED IMMEDIATELY.

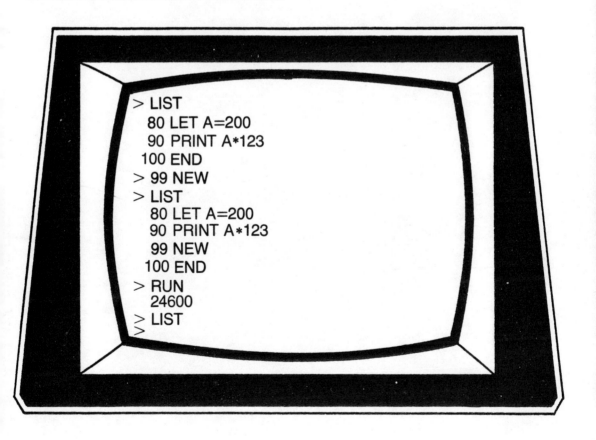

```
> LIST
  80 LET A=200
  90 PRINT A*123
 100 END
> 99 NEW
> LIST
  80 LET A=200
  90 PRINT A*123
  99 NEW
 100 END
> RUN
  24600
> LIST
>
```

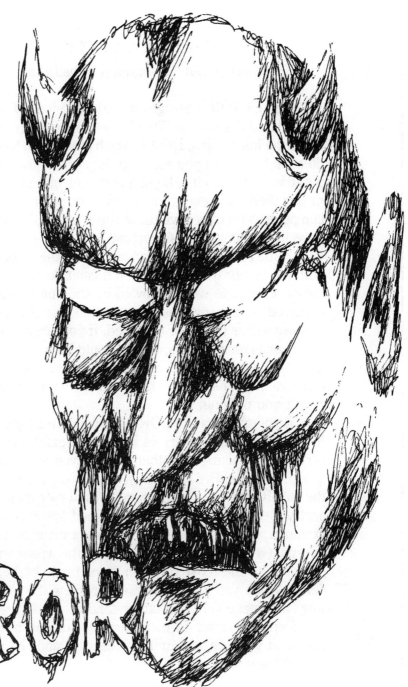

ERROR—OR "I DIDN'T DO IT!"

Yes, you did. But it's not really as bad as the cartoon makes it look.

The ERROR messages in early versions of BASIC were limited to three words: WHAT?, which means it doesn't understand the instruction; HOW?, which means you have asked it to do something, and you asked in the correct way, but the computer just can't do it (like divide by zero); and SORRY, which means there isn't enough memory to do what you asked. Some computers still only have those three words, but most BASICs have more complete information.

Some BASICs will show you the line the error occurred on, with the cursor over the section it can't do. Some give a short message or code word followed by the line number the error occurred in, and some use error numbers followed by the line number where the error occurred. If your computer uses code words or error numbers, there should be a list of these in the manual. Keep it by you and use it. It has been said that any program that runs the first time with no errors is a program that taught you nothing.

Remember that ERROR is the computer's message to you. It is used to help find errors in your program, called *bugs*, and correct them using the other powers you have learned in the group. This is called *debugging*. Once you have learned most of the BASIC powers the meaning of the error messages will be pretty clear, but one word you should know is *syntax*. As in grammer, an error in syntax or syntax error means you have misspelled a BASIC word or used it in the wrong way. This will probably be the most common error made by beginning students. When you make this error, review the section on that word and make sure you understand it.

Don't be afraid to make errors. No one has invented a computer yet with an arm that comes out and hits you if you do something wrong.

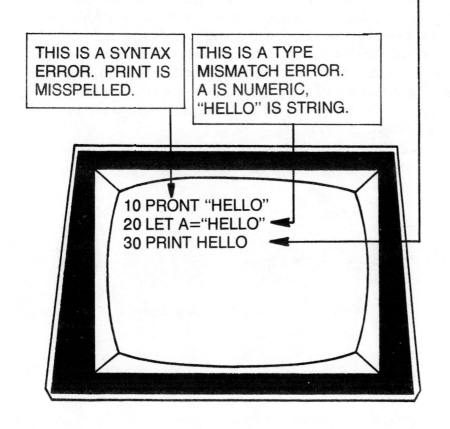

THIS IS AN EXAMPLE OF AN
ERROR THE COMPUTER CAN'T
FIND. IT WILL ASSUME HELLO
IS THE NAME OF A VARIABLE,
JUST LIKE A, B, OR C, AND PRINT
IT'S VALUE, WHICH IS ZERO IF
YOU HAVEN'T ASSIGNED IT.
IF YOUR COMPUTER DOESN'T ALLOW
VARIABLE NAMES TO BE MORE
THAN ONE OR TWO LETTERS, THIS
WILL BE A SYNTAX ERROR.

THIS IS A SYNTAX
ERROR. PRINT IS
MISSPELLED.

THIS IS A TYPE
MISMATCH ERROR.
A IS NUMERIC,
"HELLO" IS STRING.

```
10 PRONT "HELLO"
20 LET A="HELLO"
30 PRINT HELLO
```

At this point, armed with our new editing powers, you may wish to go back to the examples at the end of group 1 and do some more experimenting. Believe it or not, you now have the fundamental principles of all computing behind you. You know how to write a program, execute immediate commands (BASIC words without line numbers), and debug your programs.

You still have to learn how to input data to the computer, format output, and make the computer respond to varying situations. That is all covered in the next chapter. For now, it is time to congratulate yourself on your progress and take a break to avoid overload.

Chapter 4

Group 3

The real power of BASIC is in this group of commands. Each of them has several options that could be confusing if they are not taken slowly. None are beyond the understanding of a very young child, however, as BASIC has been successfully taught to kindergarteners. You may want to take these powers a couple at a time between rests, to avoid overload.

MATH POWERS—OR "A SUMMING UP"

This discussion of math is necessary because of the close relationship between computers and mathematics. Computers were invented to do math. The early languages, such as FORTRAN, were used as a guide when BASIC was first developed.

The main idea that has to be understood is called arithmetic hierarchy. This is another way of saying. "What order do I do the math in?" The rules are very simple.

1. Anything in parentheses is done first. If there is more than one set, they are done left to right. If the parentheses are "nested" (one set inside another set) the inner most set is done first. Math inside parentheses is done left to right.

2. After the parenthetical expressions are evaluated, the remaining math is done left to right. Exponential powers are done first.

3. Multiplication and division are on the same level and are done next.

4. Addition and subtraction are on the same level, and done last.

You should be able to deduce from this that the computer may have to make several left-to-right passes through an equation or expression before getting the answer. The expression used in the example to the right has about everything in it, and the step-by-step analysis should explain what is happening. If some of the math is beyond what you have learned, you should at least know *when* it happens, even if you don't understand *what* is happening.

5**(4/2)+2*(4*(1+2))−((10+2)/2 The two stars together, after the 5 might be / The first time through, the computer will (4/2) in parentheses and replace it with 2. It will see the (1+2) nested inside another set of parentheses and re-place it with a 3. Finally, the (10+2) will be replaced by 12.

5**2+2*(4*3)−12/2 After first pass.
Nothing after 5**2 could have a higher level, and if it were the same level it would still do this exponent first, so 5**2 (which means multiply two 5s together) is replaced by 25. Then the (4*3) is replaced by 12, and finally 12/2 is replaced by 6.

25+2*12−6 Second pass.
Since multiply and divide come before add and subtract, it will go through again and replace 2*12 with 24.

25+24−6 Third pass.
The last pass will add 25 and 24 to get 49, and then realize it can just go ahead and subtract 6 from it all in the same pass, leaving an answer of 43.

10/5*8/4 would be read by the computer as: ten divided by 5, times eight, divided by 4, or 4. If what you wanted was ten divided by 5 times eight divided by four you would write it like this 10/5*(8/4). The answer is 1. If what you wanted was ten divided by five times eight, then divided by 4 you would write 10/(5*8)/4. The answer would be 1/16 or .0625. If you want ten divided by five times eight

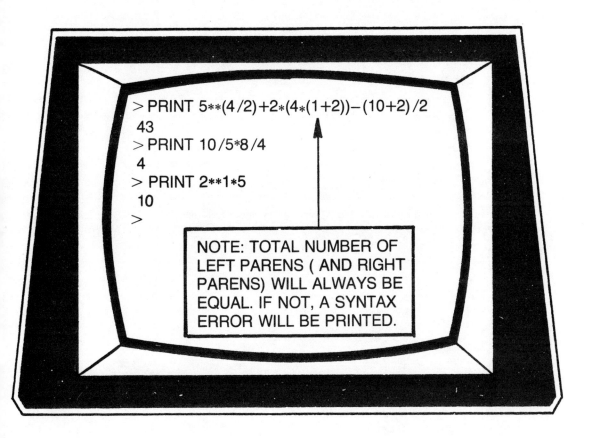

> PRINT 5**(4/2)+2*(4*(1+2))−(10+2)/2
43
> PRINT 10/5*8/4
4
> PRINT 2**1*5
10
>

NOTE: TOTAL NUMBER OF LEFT PARENS (AND RIGHT PARENS) WILL ALWAYS BE EQUAL. IF NOT, A SYNTAX ERROR WILL BE PRINTED.

divided by four you would write 10/(5*8/4). The answer is 1. As you can see, you must be very precise.

2**1*5 would be two to the first power times 5, or 10. If you wanted two to the power of one times five you would write 2**(1*5). The answer is 32.

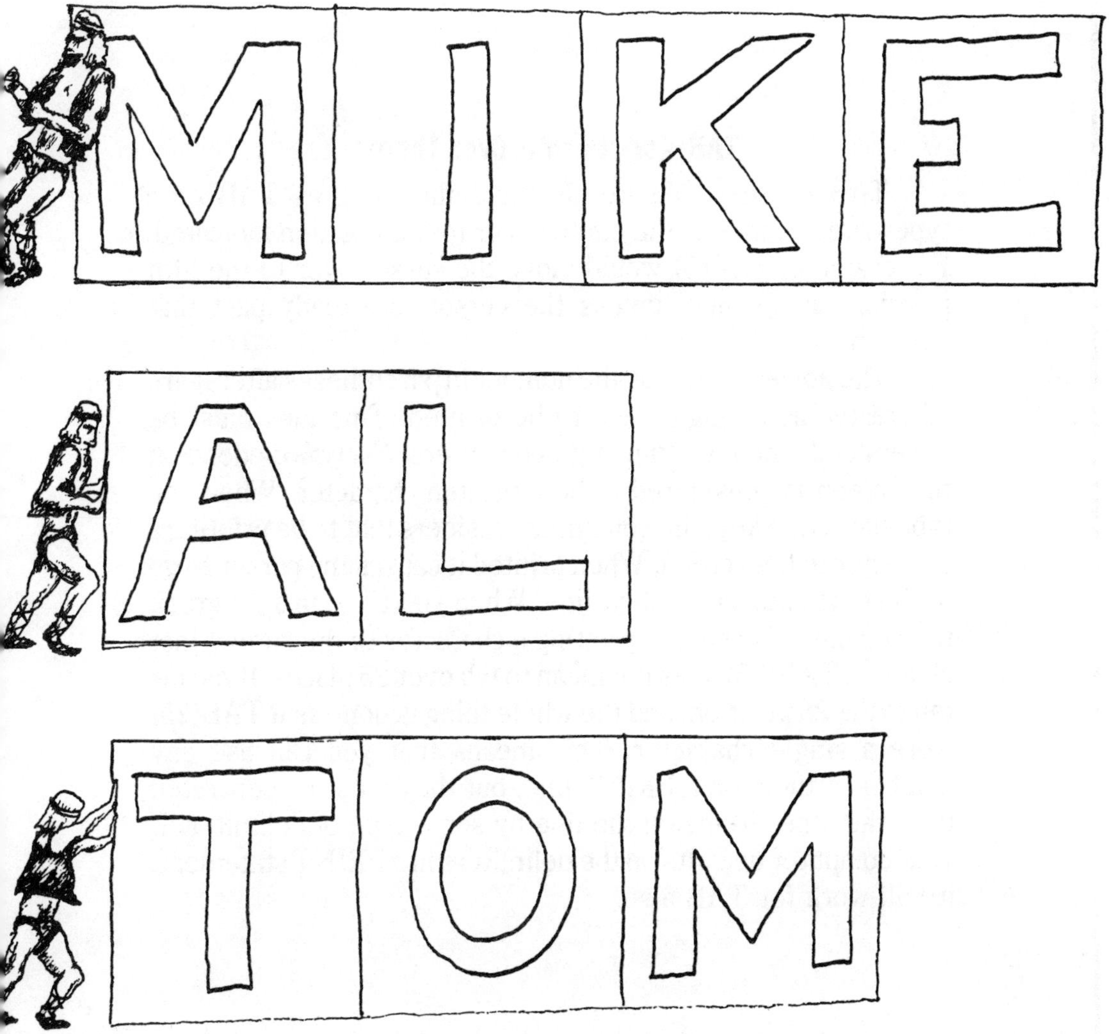
MIKE
AL
TOM

TAB—or "Push It Over There"

TAB on the computer is the same thing as TAB on a typewriter. It moves the cursor over to the position indicated. For example, TAB(5) would move the cursor over to the fifth position on the line, unless the cursor is already past that position.

The power TAB plus the number in parentheses after it are all treated as a single item to be printed. This idea must be understood when working with computers. *Everything* done on the screen is considered to be a printed character. When you type the action key, the computer considers that to be printing a character to the screen. When printed it causes the cursor to go to the beginning of the next line. When you CLS, in a program, the computer is actually printing a character to the screen that clears it. TAB(25) does not mean to tab over 25 places. It means tab to the 25 position, and the whole thing is done as if TAB(25) were a single character. This means that you can use any number of them on a PRINT line, but they must be separated from the other items on the line by some type of delimiter. If your computer defaults on the delimiters in a PRINT statement, it will work for TAB also.

10 PRINT TAB (5)"HELLO", TAB (15)"THERE" ACTION

RUN ACTION

EVERY CHARACTER TAKES THE SAME
AMOUNT OF SPACE. TAB POSITION
5 IS UNDER THE P. TAB POSITION
15 UNDER THE FIRST 5. ON MOST COMPUTERS THERE ARE
40, 64, or 80 POSITIONS TO
A LINE.

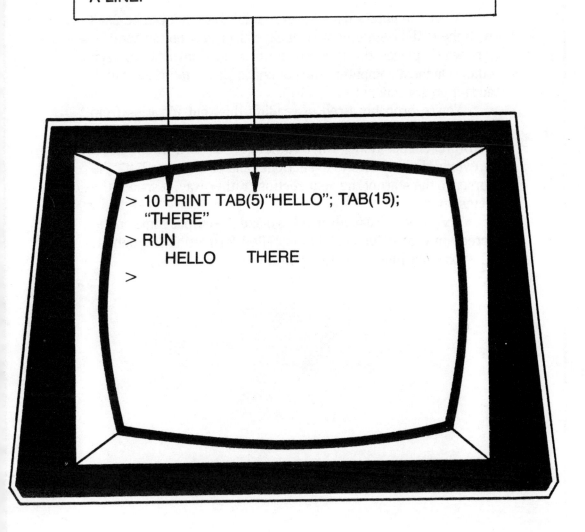

```
> 10 PRINT TAB(5)"HELLO"; TAB(15);
  "THERE"
> RUN
    HELLO     THERE
>
```

Most computers have several delimiters that can be used with the PRINT statement. You have already seen the semicolon, which places the items to be printed right next to each other. On most computers the comma is also a delimiter, but it adds a preset amount of TAB.

You're probably tired of reading this, but it varies from computer to computer. On some the comma means the same as TAB(present position + 10), on others the entire section screen is evenly divided into four sections, and the comma puts the cursor to the start of the next section. Either way, it spaces the items apart.

This power is usually used to make the output come on the screen in neat columns. This is called formatting the output. The example illustrates this point.

10 PRINT 1, 2, 3 |ACTION|

RUN |ACTION|

PRINT 1; 2, 3 |ACTION|

PRINT 1, 2, 3 |ACTION|

PRINT TAB(15)"HELLO", 4 |ACTION|

PRINT TAB(17)"HELLO", 4 |ACTION|

> NOTE THAT WHEN THE
> ITEM BEING PRINTED
> CARRIES OVER A TAB
> FIELD THE COMMA
> SPACES TO THE NEXT ONE.

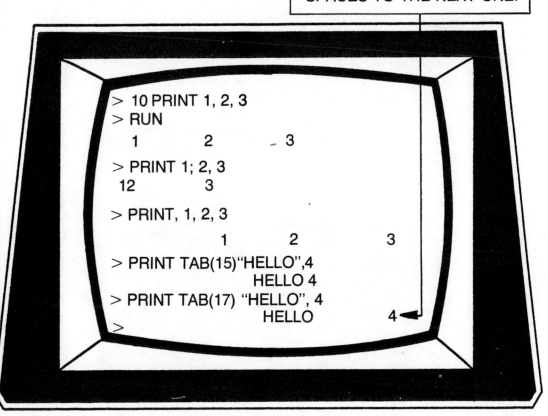

```
> 10 PRINT 1, 2, 3
> RUN
   1        2        3
> PRINT 1; 2, 3
 12        3
> PRINT, 1, 2, 3
              1        2        3
> PRINT TAB(15)"HELLO",4
              HELLO 4
> PRINT TAB(17) "HELLO", 4
              HELLO        4
>
```

INPUT—OR "GIVE IT TO ME STRAIGHT"

The INPUT power fills the gap that has existed up to this point in BASIC. That gap is the ability to give the computer information while it is running a program. This power means that the computer can do everything it needs to do and will only stop and wait for slow humans when it needs information. INPUT stops the program, usually prints a question mark on the screen, and waits for you to type in something and press the action key.

INPUT has a variable after it, and the variable is what the information you type in is stored in. The type of variable lets the computer know what to expect. Of course, if the variable is a string variable (A$) the computer will accept anything you type in, but remember that if you type in a number it will not be recognized as a number. To have your input recognized as a number use a numeric variable (A).

Besides inputting your response, to a question in a quiz for instance, the INPUT command can make your computer seem more human. An example is illustrated.

```
10 PRINT"WHAT IS YOUR NAME"
20 INPUT A$
30 PRINT "HELLO"; A$;", WOULD YOU LIKE
   TO PLAY A GAME"
40 INPUT B$
50 PRINT "YOUR WISH IS MY COMMAND"
60 END
```

RUN ACTION

DENNIS ACTION ◄──── FILL IN YOUR NAME

YES(or NO) ACTION

```
10 PRINT"HOW OLD ARE YOU";  ◄──── NOTICE THAT THE SEMICOLON
20 INPUT A                        AT THE END OF THIS PRINT
30 PRINT "WHAT YEAR IS THIS";     STATEMENT MAKES THE NEXT
40 INPUT B                        PROGRAM LINE PRINT ON
50 PRINT "YOU WERE BORN IN"; B-A  THE SAME LINE ON THE
60 END                            SCREEN.
```

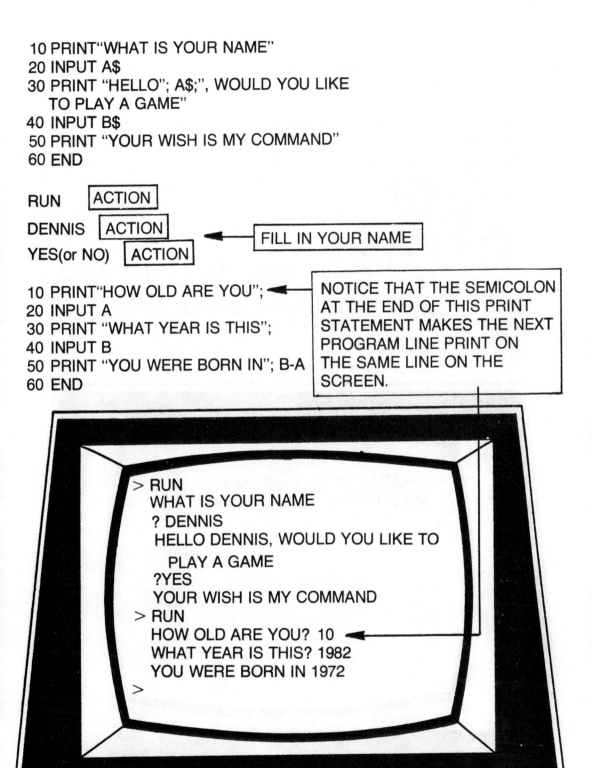

```
> RUN
  WHAT IS YOUR NAME
  ? DENNIS
  HELLO DENNIS, WOULD YOU LIKE TO
    PLAY A GAME
  ?YES
  YOUR WISH IS MY COMMAND
> RUN
  HOW OLD ARE YOU? 10  ◄────
  WHAT YEAR IS THIS? 1982
  YOU WERE BORN IN 1972
>
```

There is a form of INPUT statement that combines a PRINT with a semicolon at the end with an INPUT, and does the same thing as the two of them.

```
10 INPUT "WHAT IS YOUR NAME";A$
20 PRINT A$; "I THINK YOU'RE SMART!"
30 END
```

RUN │ ACTION │

MIKE │ ACTION │

┌─────────────────────────────┐
│ INPUT IS ONE OF THE   │
│ FEW BASIC POWERS THAT   │
│ YOU CAN'T USE WITHOUT   │
│ A LINE NUMBER!!   │
└─────────────────────────────┘

```
> RUN
  WHAT IS YOUR NAME? MIKE
  MIKE, I THINK YOU'RE SMART!
>
```

GOTO

GOTO—OR "ONE WAY TICKET"

As we said at the very beginning of this book, BASIC is a very simple language in which most of the words mean the same thing they mean in English. The same is true of the GOTO power. GOTO where? BASIC identifies statements by line number, so the line numbers are an obvious guess, and you'd be right. The number after the GOTO must be a line number of the program. If the number is of a non-existent line, an error will occur.

You may have already discovered that when you type RUN all of the variables are reset before the program is run. To get the program to start running *without* resetting all the variables, you can type GOTO and use the first line number of the program. In fact, you may pick any line number of the program, as long as you are sure you are not jumping into a place that will cause a later error.

```
10 CLS
20 PRINT "MY NAME IS COMPUTER"
30 INPUT"WHAT IS YOUR NAME?"; A$
40 PRINT "THAT'S NICE"; A$
50 PRINT "NOW, IF THERE IS ANYONE ELSE IN THE
   ROOM,"
60 GOTO 30
70 END
```

RUN   ACTION

MARY   ACTION

JOHN   ACTION
:
:

BREAK

```
MY NAME IS COMPUTER
WHAT IS YOUR NAME? MARY
THAT'S NICE MARY
NOW, IF THERE IS ANYONE ELSE IN THE
   ROOM,
WHAT IS YOUR NAME? JOHN
THAT'S NICE JOHN
NOW, IF THERE IS ANYONE ELSE IN THE
   ROOM,
WHAT IS YOUR NAME?
BREAK IN LINE 40
>
```

IF . . . THEN—or "The Deciding Factor"

IF . . . THEN is the last of the great BASIC powers that you must know to do modern computing. The GOTO power branched the program to a new location regardless of the circumstances. This is called an unconditional branching. The IF . . . THEN allows you to check certain conditions and branch or not branch accordingly. This is called conditional branching. If a machine can store a program, manipulate data (usually the math powers), do input and output, and support conditional branching, it is a computer, no matter what shape or form it takes.

Testing the condition takes two forms. The first is arithmetic. Any numeric variable or numeric expression can be put between the IF and the THEN. If the value of that expression or variable is zero then the computer just goes on to the next line number. If it is not zero, the action differs with different computers. In most computers *any* answer other than zero is enough to send the computer to the THEN statement. On other computers a negative answer is like a zero, and only the positive answer sends the computer to the THEN. You will have to experiment to see which your computer does. The experiment is illustrated.

```
80 INPUT "TYPE A NUMBER";2
90 IF Z THEN GOTO 120
100 PRINT Z; "DOESN'T BRANCH"
110 GOTO 80
120 PRINT Z;"DOES BRANCH"
130 GOTO 80
```

THE ANSWER
HERE WILL TELL
IF NEGATIVE
NUMBERS BRANCH ON
YOUR COMPUTER.

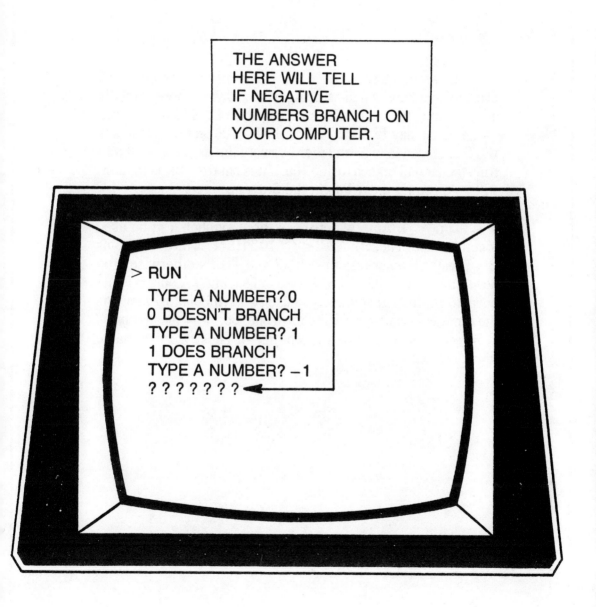

```
> RUN
TYPE A NUMBER? 0
0 DOESN'T BRANCH
TYPE A NUMBER? 1
1 DOES BRANCH
TYPE A NUMBER? −1
? ? ? ? ? ? ?
```

The second form of IF . . . THEN is used more often and evaluates an expression as being true or false. Three symbols are used in these expressions. The first is our old friend equals (=). You can say IF A=2 THEN GOTO 100 and the computer will find the value of A, and then evaluate the expression. If it is true, then it will branch to line 100. If it is not true, the computer will go on to the next line in the program.

The other two symbols are the greater than (>) and the less than (<). Any two of these three symbols can be used together, also. Thus, IF A+B< >10 THEN . . . means if A plus B is greater than or less than 10 do the THEN otherwise drop down to the next line. This is a way of saying if A plus B is not equal to 10. In fact, anytime you use two symbols together it is the same as saying it is *not* the third one. So, > = means *not* <, < = means *not* >, and < > means *not* =. These work the same on all computers.

```
10 PRINT "HOW MUCH IS 1+1?"
20 INPUT A
30 IF A=2 THEN GOTO 60
40 PRINT "WRONG"
50 GOTO 10
60 PRINT "RIGHT"
70 END
```

REMEMBER! IF YOU ARE WRONG WHEN YOU WRITE THE PROGRAM, THE COMPUTER WILL BE TOO!

```
 5 PRINT "ANSWER TRUE OR FALSE"
10 PRINT "BIRDS HAVE WINGS"
20 INPUT A$
30 IF A$= "TRUE" THEN GOTO 60
40 PRINT "WRONG"
50 END
60 PRINT "RIGHT!"
70 END
```

NOTICE THE NEW USE OF END. SINCE THE ANSWER CAN ONLY BE TRUE OR FALSE A SECOND CHANCE IS NOT NEEDED. THIS END KEEPS LINES 60 AND 70 FROM BEING RUN AFTER WRONG IS PRINTED.

IF YOUR COMPUTER DOESN'T ALLOW TWO ENDS MAKE LINE 70 GOTO 50.

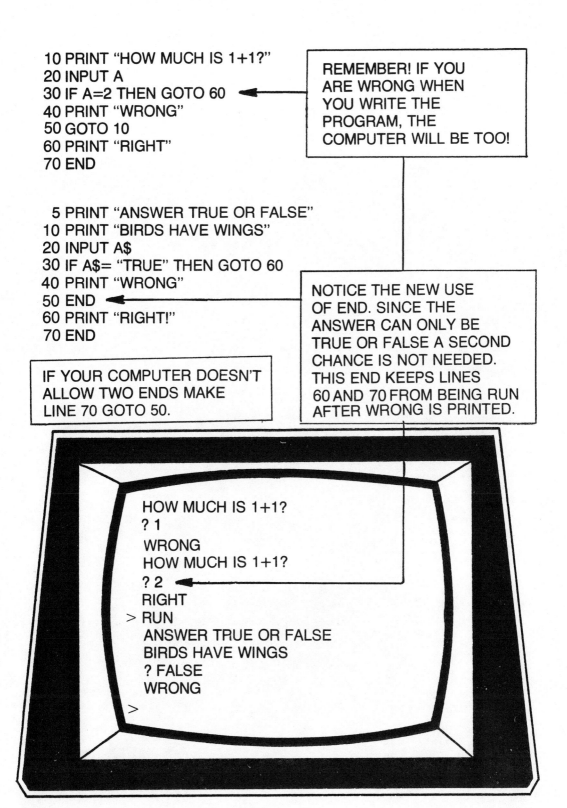

```
HOW MUCH IS 1+1?
? 1
WRONG
HOW MUCH IS 1+1?
? 2
RIGHT
> RUN
ANSWER TRUE OR FALSE
BIRDS HAVE WINGS
? FALSE
WRONG
>
```

RANDOM—or "The Riverboat Gambler"

At this point you have already learned all of the BASIC powers you really need to do most of your computing. The rest of these powers are just faster or easier ways of doing some of these commonly used routines. RANDOM generates random numbers. This means you don't know in advance what the number will be. It is used in games and some simulations (where you make the computer act like some other machine). First, let's look at how random numbers *could* de done.

We have mentioned exponents a few times, and even though these may be beyond what you have learned in math, there is one example anyone should be able to grasp. 10 to any power is the same as putting that many zeros after 1. For example 10^4 is 10000 and 10^7 is 10000000. In all computers 10 to a power is expressed as a capital E followed by the power symbol, so 10^7 is E7. Multiplying a number by a power of 10 is the same as moving the decimal point that many places to the right, so E3 times 1.2345 is 1234.5

Now, suppose your computer only does math to 7 decimal places. The eight place is in memory, but it is not accurate and varies. If you multiply that number by E7, chop off the top part, and multiply the result by any number you will get a random number somewhere between zero and the final number you multiplied by. The example shows this.

There are two problems with this. Steps 30, 40, and 50 could take a long time, and the range isn't very big. It will vary by only a few numbers. If you do it several times and use the INT power it will work. The second example demonstrates this.

```
5 PRINT "YOUR RANDOM NUMBER WILL BE GREATER THAN ZERO"
6 INPUT "WHAT NUMBER SHOULD IT BE LESS THAN";C

10 INPUT "TYPE IN A NUMBER";A
20 B=A / 13*1E7        ◀——  THIS GETS A DECIMAL NUMBER
                            AND MULTIPLIES BEYOND ACCURACY
30 B=B−1
40 IF B<1 THEN GOTO 60 ◀——  THIS CUTS OFF THE TOP BY SUBTRACTING
                            UNTIL ANSWER<1.
50 GOTO 30
60 A=B*C               ◀——  MULTIPLIES TO MAKE IT THE RIGHT SIZE

70 PRINT INT(A)        ◀——  INT IS A POWER THAT CHOPS OFF THE
                            DECIMAL POINTS.
80 END

5 INPUT "WHAT IS THE UPPER LIMIT OF RANDOM";C
10 INPUT "TYPE IN A NUMBER";A
20 I=1
30 B=A / 13*1E7
40 A=B−INT(B)          ◀——  INT(B) CHOPS OFF THE DECIMAL
                            LEAVING TOP, SO
50 I=I+1                    B-INT(B) IS JUST THE DECIMAL

60 IF I<6 THEN GOTO 30 ◀——  I IS A COUNTER. THE BIGGER YOU
70 B=A*C                    MAKE THE NUMBER THE MORE TIMES
80 PRINT INT(B)             THE LOOP RUNS.
90 END
```

L
O
O
P

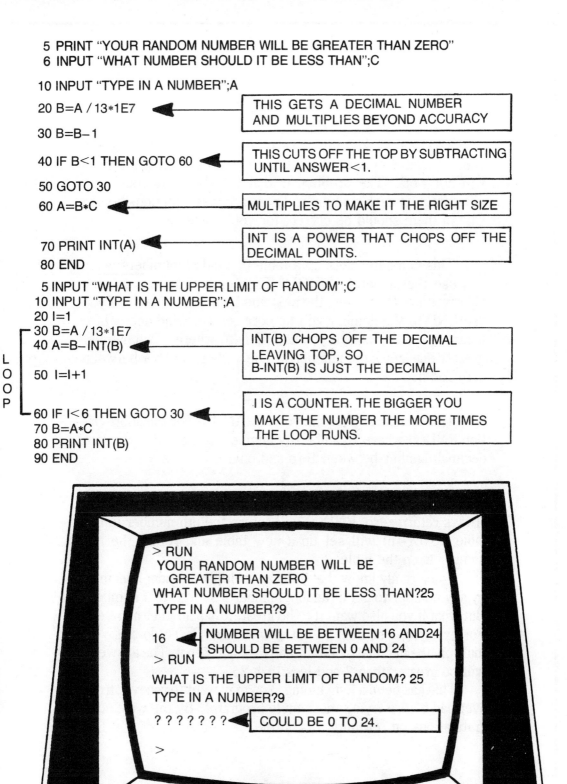

```
> RUN
 YOUR RANDOM NUMBER WILL BE
   GREATER THAN ZERO
WHAT NUMBER SHOULD IT BE LESS THAN?25
TYPE IN A NUMBER?9

16  ◀——  NUMBER WILL BE BETWEEN 16 AND 24
          SHOULD BE BETWEEN 0 AND 24
> RUN

WHAT IS THE UPPER LIMIT OF RANDOM? 25
TYPE IN A NUMBER?9

? ? ? ? ? ? ?  ◀——  COULD BE 0 TO 24.

>
```

93

RANDOM takes the place of all of that. Furthermore, if your computer only does integer numbers the program given will not work. The problem is that RANDOM is done very differently on each computer. There are three sections below. One of them should be correct for your machine.

1

This computer sets up a table of random numbers when you use the power RANDOM. Then each time you use the abbreviation RND it gets the next number from the table. If you use RND(0) the number will be between zero and one, which means it is a decimal. If you use RND(n) where n is a number greater than zero, the number will be a whole number between zero and n.

2

This computer uses the power RANDOM or the abbreviation RND(x) where x can be any number and returns a random decimal number between zero and one.

3

This computer has a table in memory already. RND(0) will always return zero. RND(n) will return the nth number in the table. RND(−n) will set up a new table and return the nth number from the table.

You already know that you can multiply a random decimal by any number to get a random number less than that number. But what if you also want it to be greater than another number? For example, less than 25 but greater than 7? To do this you multiply the decimal by 25−7, and then add 7 to it. The answers will be greater than 7 and less than 25.

This has been a long inning. You may want to recover from overload before trying the sample programs. By the way, congratulations on reaching this hurdle.

Group 3 Sample Programs

Remember, never be satisfied to just type in a program and get it running. Always make it a rule to change things in a program after it does run. This is the best way to learn how to build programs. Read these sample programs carefully, as some new concepts are presented in them.

```
10 PRINT "THIS PROGRAM CONVERTS INCHES TO
    FEET"
20 PRINT "HOW MANY INCHES";
30 INPUT C
40 LET X=INT (C/12)  ◄── AT 12 INCHES PER FOOT X = EXACT NUMBER
                           OF FEET WITH NO REMAINDER

50 LET P=C−X*12  ◄── EXACT FEET *12 IS EXACT INCHES
                      SUBTRACTED FROM TOTAL=REMAINDER
60 PRINT
70 PRINT C; "INCHES = ";X; "FEET ";P;"INCHES"
80 END
```

THE SAMPLE RUN SHOWS
NEED FOR IMPROVEMENT. TRY
USING IF . . . THEN TO CORRECT
THE PROBLEMS.

```
> RUN
  THIS PROGRAM CONVERTS INCHES TO
    FEET
  HOW MANY INCHES?25
  25 INCHES=2 FEET 1 INCH
> RUN
  THIS PROGRAM CONVERTS INCHES TO
    FEET
  HOW MANY INCHES?12
  12 INCHES=1 FEET 0 INCHES
>
```

```
10 PRINT "MULTIPLICATION QUIZ"
20 INPUT "WHAT IS YOUR FIRST NAME ";A$

30 CLS
40 LET A=INT(10*RND(0))
50 LET B=INT(10*RND(0))+10
60 PRINT A;"*";B;"=";
70 INPUT C
80 IF C=A*B THEN GOTO 140
90 PRINT "WRONG";A$;", TRY AGAIN."

100 I=1
110 I=I+1
120 IF I< 100 THEN GOTO 110
130 GOTO 60
140 PRINT "GOOD WORK ";A$"!"
150 I=1
160 I=I+1
170 IF I< 100 THEN GOTO 160
180 GOTO 30
190 END
```

CHANGE TO WHATEVER CLEARS THE SCREEN ON YOUR COMPUTER.

THESE LINES DO NOTHING BUT DELAY LONG ENOUGH FOR YOU TO READ THE SCREEN. YOU CAN CHANGE THE NUMBER 100 TO WHATEVER YOU LIKE.

RANDOM VALUES APPEAR HERE. THE FIRST BETWEEN 0 AND 9, THE SECOND BETWEEN 10 AND 19.

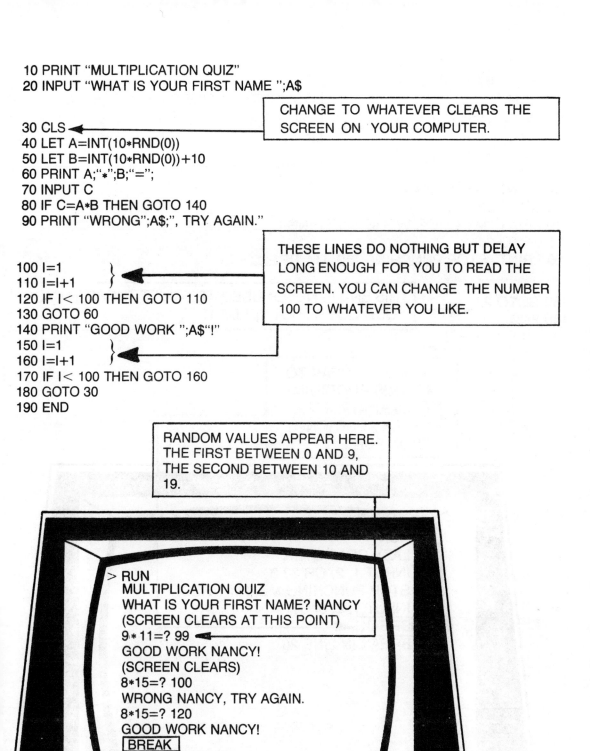

```
> RUN
MULTIPLICATION QUIZ
WHAT IS YOUR FIRST NAME? NANCY
(SCREEN CLEARS AT THIS POINT)
9*11=? 99
GOOD WORK NANCY!
(SCREEN CLEARS)
8*15=? 100
WRONG NANCY, TRY AGAIN.
8*15=? 120
GOOD WORK NANCY!
 BREAK
> BREAK IN 170 (OR 160)
```

```
10 PRINT "LAZY COMPUTER"
20 PRINT "INPUT 1, 2, OR 3";
30 INPUT L
40 IF L=1 THEN GOTO 100
50 IF L=2 THEN GOTO 110
60 IF L=3 THEN GOTO 120
```

COMPUTER DROPS THRU THE LIST UNTIL RIGHT VALUE FOR L IS FOUND. IF L<> 1, 2, OR 3 COMPUTER DOES LINE 100.

```
100 PRINT "WHO TURNED ME ON?"
105 GOTO 20
110 PRINT "MY CHIPS WERE SLEEPING!"
115 GOTO 20
120 PRINT "STOP PUNCHING ME, I'M TIRED!"

130 GOTO 20
140 END
```

THIS END IS NEVER USED. IT IS JUST THERE IN CASE YOUR COMPUTER NEEDS IT.

YOU MUST BREAK TO EXIT THIS PROGRAM. TRY MAKING IT END WITH AN ADDITIONAL OPTION FOR L.

```
> RUN
LAZY COMPUTER
INPUT 1, 2, OR 3? 3
STOP PUNCHING ME, I'M TIRED!
INPUT 1, 2, or 3?
BREAK
BREAK IN LINE 20.
>
```

TRADITIONAL WAY
```
10 PRINT "PARCEL RATES"
20 INPUT "INPUT POUNDS";A
30  IF A > = 50 THEN GOTO 90
40  IF A > = 40 THEN GOTO 120
50  IF A > = 30 THEN GOTO 140
60  IF A > = 20 THEN GOTO 160
70  IF A > = 10 THEN GOTO 180
80  IF A > = 1 THEN GOTO 200
90  PRINT "PARCEL REJECTED"
100 GOTO 10
120 PRINT "$20"
130 GOTO 10
140 PRINT "$15"
150 GOTO 10
160 PRINT "$10"
170 GOTO 10
180 PRINT "$5"
190 GOTO 10
200 PRINT "$1"
210 GOTO 10
220 END
```

A BETTER WAY
```
10 PRINT "PARCEL RATES"
20 INPUT "INPUT POUNDS";A
30 IF A = > 50 THEN GOTO 90
40 LET A=5*INT (A/ 10)
45 IF A < 25 THEN GOTO 50
46 LET A = 20
50 IF A=0 THEN GOTO 80
60 PRINT "$";A
70 GOTO 10
80 PRINT "$1"
85 GOTO 10
90 PRINT "PARCEL REJECTED"
100 GOTO 10
110 END
```

BOTH RUN THE SAME.

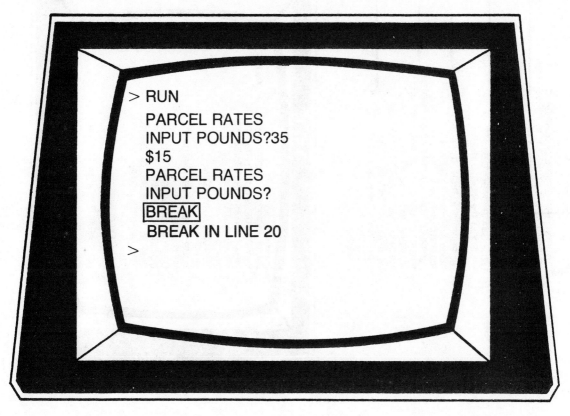

```
> RUN
  PARCEL RATES
  INPUT POUNDS?35
  $15
  PARCEL RATES
  INPUT POUNDS?
  BREAK
  BREAK IN LINE 20
>
```

HERE IS THE TECHNIQUE DISCUSSED FOR GETTING A RANDOM DECIMAL INTO A RANGE. ADD THE WORD RANDOM TO THE FRONT OF THIS LINE IF YOU CAN.

MORE THAN ONE STATEMENT CAN BE PUT ON A LINE IF THE STATEMENTS ARE SEPARATED BY A COLON. ONE COMPUTER REQUIRES TWO COLONS AND SOME MAY NOT SUPPORT THIS FEATURE AT ALL IF NOT ADD EXTRA LINES.

THIS ERROR TRAPPING ROUTINE MAKES SURE THAT EITHER Y OR N IS TYPED BEFORE THE BRANCH IS MADE. ANY OTHER ANSWERS WILL LOOP THE PROGRAM BACK TO THE QUESTION.

```
10 PRINT "I HAVE PICKED A NUMBER BETWEEN 1 AND 25"
20 PRINT "TRY TO GUESS IT IN THREE TRIES"
30 LET A=INT(25*RND(0))+1
35 Y=0
40 PRINT "WHAT IS YOUR FIRST GUESS";
50 INPUT G: LET Y=Y+1
60 IF G=A THEN GOTO 90
65 IF Y=3 THEN GOTO 190
70 IF G < A THEN GOTO 150
80 PRINT "TOO HIGH. TRY AGAIN": GOTO 50
90 PRINT "RIGHT! YOU WIN!"
100 GOTO 200
150 PRINT "TOO LOW. TRY AGAIN": GOTO 50
190 PRINT "YOUR THREE TRIES ARE UP"
200 PRINT "MY NUMBER WAS ",A
210 INPUT "DO IT AGAIN? Y OR N",A$
220 IF A$="Y" THEN GOTO 30
230 IF A$="N"THEN GOTO 250
240 GOTO 210
250 END
```

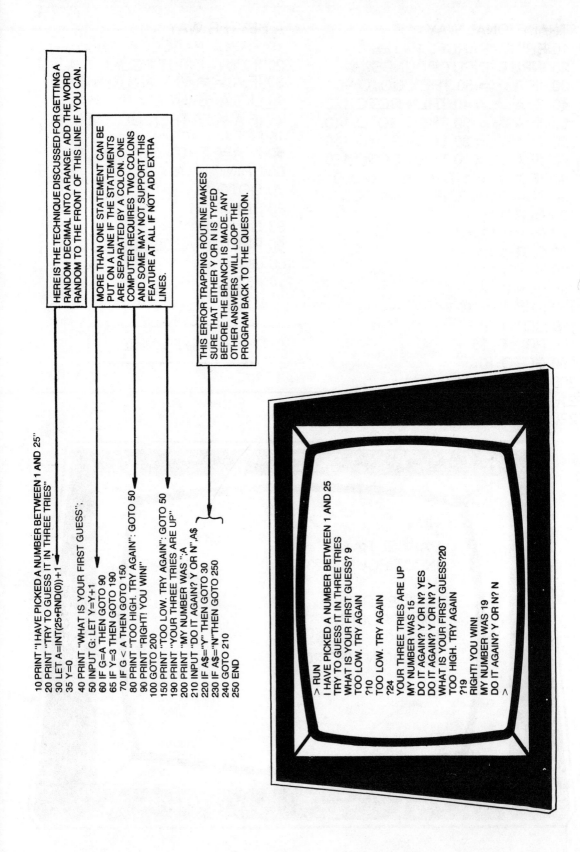

```
> RUN
I HAVE PICKED A NUMBER BETWEEN 1 AND 25
TRY TO GUESS IT IN THREE TRIES
WHAT IS YOUR FIRST GUESS? 9
TOO LOW. TRY AGAIN
?10
TOO LOW. TRY AGAIN
?24
YOUR THREE TRIES ARE UP
MY NUMBER WAS 15
DO IT AGAIN? Y OR N? YES
DO IT AGAIN? Y OR N? Y
WHAT IS YOUR FIRST GUESS?20
TOO HIGH. TRY AGAIN
?19
RIGHT! YOU WIN!
MY NUMBER WAS 19
DO IT AGAIN? Y OR N? N
>
```

Chapter 5

Group 4

This last group consists of two pairs of words that duplicates what you can already do in BASIC but allow you to do it faster and with fewer program lines. Each pair must be used together, like IF . . . THEN, but each power in the pair is a separate statement and does not have to appear on the same line.

When you finish this group, you will find two sets of programs. The first concentrates on these two pairs of words so that you can master them, and the second group covers everything you have learned up to that point. You will be amazed to discover that you are capable of some rather complex programming.

FOR / NEXT—OR "BRING IN THE MULE"

You may wonder about the odd nick-name for this pair. After you have used it for a while, the mystery will clear up. This will probably be the most important power you use, and you will probably use it as often as the PRINT power.

You are already familiar with the first example of looping given. The index variable (I in the example, but it can be any numeric variable) is set and then incremented as part of the loop. When its value causes the test to fail, you come out of the loop. FOR / NEXT allows you to do the same thing but is faster and could save you up to half the program space needed to store the Index variable / GOTO type of loop. In addition it can be done on a single line if necessary, whereas the Index variable / GOTO loop cannot.

```
10 I= 0
20 PRINT "MARY"
30 I=I+1
40 IF I< 3 THEN GOTO 20
50 END

10 FOR I=1 TO 3
20 PRINT "MARY"
30 NEXT I
40 END

10 PRINT "HELLO": FOR I=1 TO 3: PRINT "MARY":NEXT
   I:END
```

THE NEXT STATEMENT LOOPS BACK TO THE FOR STATEMENT WHICH DOESN'T HAVE TO BE AT THE BEGINNING OF A LINE.

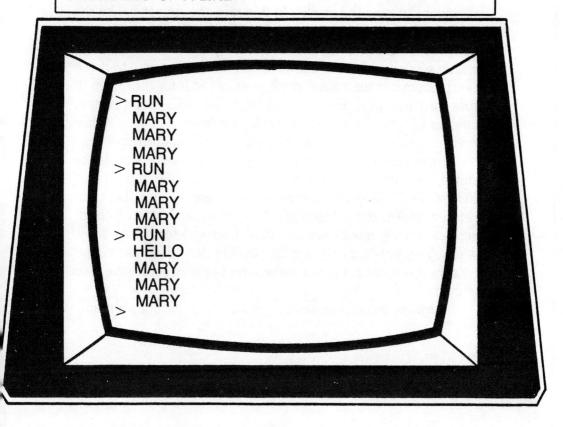

```
> RUN
  MARY
  MARY
  MARY
> RUN
  MARY
  MARY
  MARY
> RUN
  HELLO
  MARY
  MARY
  MARY
>
```

Just as you can nest parentheses, you can nest loops. These may be mixed between Index variable / GOTO loops and FOR / NEXT loops, but most of the time it is advantageous to use FOR / NEXT loops. When nesting loops, the inside loop, which loops through fewer instructions, is done faster. It goes through its complete cycle once; then the outside loop is incremented and the inside loop goes through a complete cycle again. This continues until the outside loop has been completed.

Let's use an illustration drawn from the cartoon. Suppose we have a two-person relay team. The first person runs around the track with the baton. Just as they near the end of the track they must mark the baton with chalk, then pass the baton to the second person. If the baton has the required number of chalk marks to complete the race then the race is over, but only the receiver can read the marks. In this race the runner is like the FOR and the receiver is like the NEXT. Now let's suppose that half way around the track there are two more team members with a second, different, baton. When the runner gets to these two team mates the runner must stop and wait for these two to toss the baton they have back and forth to each other a certain number of times. The tosser marks the baton and the catcher reads the number of marks. When the catcher determines that the proper number of marks is on the baton he or she signals the runner to continue. This second group is like the nested FOR / NEXT loop. Each time a runner approaches them the referee wipes their baton clean so they are starting from scratch. If they must toss the baton back and forth four times when a runner is waiting, and the runners must do five laps, the tossers end up tossing their baton twenty times before the race is over.

Perhaps this can be seen by updating an earlier program.

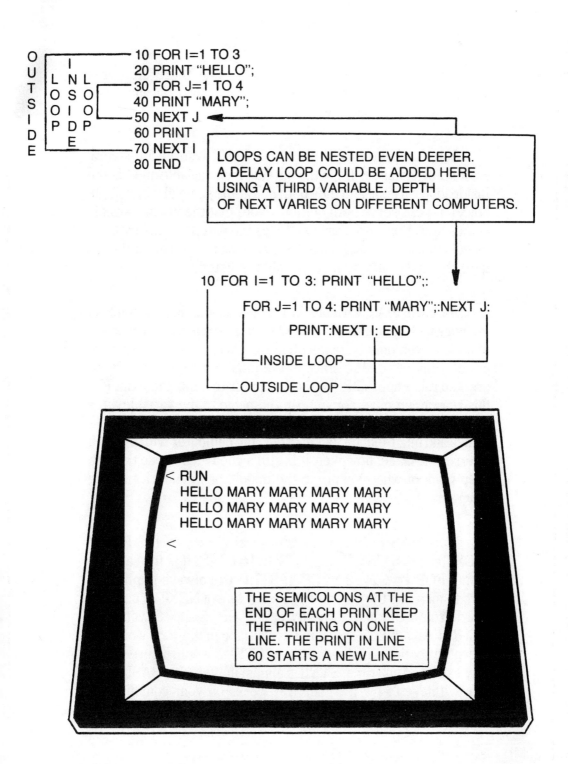

```
OUTSIDE LOOP    INSIDE LOOP
                            10 FOR I=1 TO 3
                            20 PRINT "HELLO";
                            30 FOR J=1 TO 4
                            40 PRINT "MARY";
                            50 NEXT J
                            60 PRINT
                            70 NEXT I
                            80 END
```

LOOPS CAN BE NESTED EVEN DEEPER.
A DELAY LOOP COULD BE ADDED HERE
USING A THIRD VARIABLE. DEPTH
OF NEXT VARIES ON DIFFERENT COMPUTERS.

```
10 FOR I=1 TO 3: PRINT "HELLO";:

    FOR J=1 TO 4: PRINT "MARY";:NEXT J:

        PRINT:NEXT I: END

        └INSIDE LOOP──────┘

    └───OUTSIDE LOOP────┘
```

```
< RUN
HELLO MARY MARY MARY MARY
HELLO MARY MARY MARY MARY
HELLO MARY MARY MARY MARY

<
```

THE SEMICOLONS AT THE
END OF EACH PRINT KEEP
THE PRINTING ON ONE
LINE. THE PRINT IN LINE
60 STARTS A NEW LINE.

Before leaving the FOR / NEXT loop there are three things you need to know. These are left to last because they vary in different computers.

1

Some computers will allow one NEXT to serve for several FORs. For instance, if I is the outside loop variable and J is the inside loop variable and they both end at the same place, a single NEXT J, I can serve both of them. Note that the inside variable comes first. For more than two loops the pattern holds with the most inside loops being listed first then the next on out and so on until the most outside loop variable is listed.

2

As each FOR variable is read, it is put into a stack of memory with each successive FOR variable pushed down on top of it. They can only be taken off in the reverse order they were put on (top one on the stack is the most inside and comes off first) so it is impossible for the computer to mess them up. For this reason, on most computers, the name of the variable after the NEXT is not really necessary. If you *do* use the variable names and mix them up, out of order, the computer will give you an error message; however, it is still a good idea to use them to keep track of what you are in the middle of when writing long programs.

3

Most BASICs allow an additional power to the FOR / NEXT called STEP. If you say FOR I=1 TO 3 it is the same as saying FOR I=1 TO 3 STEP 1. STEP 1 is always implied. It says to increase the variable by 1 each time a NEXT is encountered. You could just as easily say STEP .5 and .5 would be added at each NEXT, meaning everything in the loop would be executed six times instead of three. STEP 3 would insure that it only executed one time. STEP is almost universal in BASIC, but you will have to try it to see if it works on your computer.

READ / DATA—or "On the Look-Out"

READ is constantly on the look-out for DATA. So much so that it will generate an error if it can't find any or if there isn't enough. READ will search across every line in the program looking for DATA. It will remember the last piece of DATA it read and remember where to look for the next piece. READ isn't prejudiced either. It will look for either string DATA or numeric DATA just as you instruct it to. And it does it much faster than you could ever type it in with INPUT.

The example is a quiz in biology. With READ / DATA all I have to do is type in a new DATA statement and I have a whole new quiz! Even in a different topic!

```
  5 W=0                    ┌─────────────────────────────────────────────────┐
 10 R=0                    │ READ AND INPUT CAN BOTH HAVE MORE THAN ONE      │
 15 CLS                    │ VARIABLE                                        │
 20 READ A$, B$  ◀─────────┘
 30 PRINT "GIVE THE PROPER";A$;"OF EACH";B$
 40 FOR I=1 TO 10
 50 READ A$, B$
 60 PRINT A$;
 70 INPUT C$
 80 IF B$=C$ THEN GOTO 120      ┌──────────────────────────────┐
 90 PRINT "WRONG. IT IS ";B$    │ MOST COMPUTERS ALLOW YOU     │
                                │ TO LEAVE OFF THE LET.        │
 95 W=W+1  ◀────────────────────┘
                                        ┌──────────────────────┐
100 NEXT I                              │ AVERAGE * 100= %     │
110 PRINT "YOU SCORED "; 100*R/(R+W);" PERCENT  ◀──────────────┘
115 END  ◀───────┤ NOTICE WHERE THE END IS │
120 PRINT "CORRECT!"     ┌────────────────────────────────────────────┐
125 R=R+1                │ DATA MAY BE ON ANY NUMBER OF LINES,        │
130 GOTO 100             │ SEPARATED BY COMMAS. NOTICE MAPLE          │
                         │ TREE. YOU MAY IMBED SPACES                 │
200 DATA KINGDOM, ITEM  ◀┘
210 DATA TROUT, ANIMAL, TOMATO, VEGETABLE,
      BLUEJAY, ANIMAL
220 DATA DIAMOND, MINERAL, MAPLE TREE, VEGET-
      ABLE, BEE, ANIMAL  ◀─────────────────────────┘
230  DATA IRON, MINERAL. GRASS, VEGETABLE, LEM-
      ON, VEGETABLE
240 DATA SPARROW, ANIMAL
```

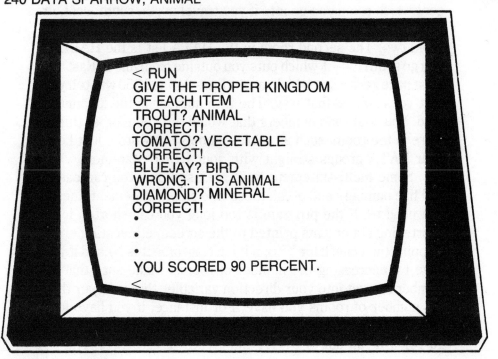

```
< RUN
GIVE THE PROPER KINGDOM
OF EACH ITEM
TROUT? ANIMAL
CORRECT!
TOMATO? VEGETABLE
CORRECT!
BLUEJAY? BIRD
WRONG. IT IS ANIMAL
DIAMOND? MINERAL
CORRECT!
 .
 .
 .
YOU SCORED 90 PERCENT.
<
```

String and numeric arguments can be mixed in DATA statements as long as you take care that your READ statements keep everything straight. The example here is part of the code for an adventure game.

Your world consists of a series of locations and what is at those locations. Through short commands you can direct your character to pick up, drop, or use objects that you find; travel in certain directions; eat; fight; or flee in terror. You see, your world is usually populated with random nasties out to get you. Your objective is to find treasure or kill the monster or to just get out alive.

You should be aware of a new power as you work with this example. RESTORE replaces the DATA pointer back to the front of the first DATA statement in the program.

There are five places in the house presented here. P is a variable that tells which room you are in. G tells how much gold you have. T tells how much gold is in the room. If it equals 10, it means there is a monster in the room. You could then generate T randomly each time a room is entered. This would make the monster appear random also, thus increasing the excitement.

The READ, in line 12, says to read a string variable and five numeric ones. Each group of data in the DATA statements has a string (the room) and five numeric values. The first four represent which room you go into if you travel north, south, east, or west. So in position 1, the front door, if you go north you are in room two. The second room in the DATA list is the HALL. If you go south P=−1 which puts you outside from line 5. East and west have zero value which means lines 348 and 350 will tell you that you can't go that way. The fifth number is the amount of gold. You could add numbers that would tell you if other things were in the room, such as secret tunnels or swords. Just keep your DATA groups straight with your READ statement.

Some multi-statement lines are used, but you can easily add line numbers and break these into single statement lines if you need to. If the program is too long you can shorten it by shortening statements printed to the screen, eliminating error trapping (just check for YES; if it isn't, assume it is N), and if you have to, decreasing the number of rooms. Make sure that no number can get into your direction variables that is larger than the number of rooms you have. For instance, if you have four rooms and north says go to room six, the READ loop (lines 10-14) will run out of DATA and create an error.

```
  1 P=1:G=0
  3 RESTORE
  5 IF P=-1 THEN GOTO 1000
 10 FOR I=1 TO P
 12 READ A$, N,S,E,W,T
 14 NEXT I
 20 PRINT "YOU ARE IN THE ";A$;". THERE IS A DOOR TO THE ";
 30 IF N=0 THEN GOTO 34
 32 PRINT "-N";
 34 IF S=0 THEN GOTO 38
 36 PRINT "-S";
 38 IF E=0 THEN GOTO 42
 40 PRINT "-E";
 42 IF W=0 THEN GOTO 46
 44 PRINT "-W";
 46 PRINT
100 IF T=0 THEN GOTO 200
105 IF T=10 THEN GOTO 500
110 PRINT "YOU SEE ";T;" PIECES OF GOLD!"
200 INPUT "WHAT DO YOU WANT TO DO";B$
210 IF B$<> "GET" THEN GOTO 290
220 IF T>0 THEN GOTO 250
230 PRINT "THERE ISN'T ANYTHING HERE!":GOTO 200
250 PRINT "OK":G=G+T:T=0:GOTO 200
290 IF B$= "GO" THEN GOTO 320
300 PRINT "I DON'T UNDERSTAND YOU":GOTO 200
320 INPUT "WHICH DIRECTION ";B$
322 IF B$="N" THEN GOTO 346
324 IF B$="S" THEN GOTO 342
326 IF B$="E" THEN GOTO 338
328 IF B$="W" THEN GOTO 334
330 PRINT "WHAT?":GOTO 320
334 P=W:GOTO 348
338: P=E:GOTO 348
342 P=S:GOTO 348
346 P=N
348 IF P<>0 THEN GOTO 3
350 PRINT "I CAN'T GO THAT WAY!": GOTO 320
500 PRINT "YOU HAVE ENTERED THE ROOM WITH THE MONSTER"
510 PRINT "AND HE EATS YOU":END
1000 PRINT "YOU MADE IT OUT ALIVE WITH ";G;"PIECES OF GOLD."
1010 INPUT "WANT TO GO BACK FOR MORE ";B$
1020 IF B$<> "Y" THEN GOTO 2000
1030 P=1:GOTO 3
1500 DATA FRONT DOOR, 2, -1, 0, 0, 0, HALL, 3, 1, 4, 5, 1, DINING ROOM, 0, 2,
     4, 5, 2
1510 DATA BALL ROOM, 3, 0, 0, 2, 1, DEN, 3, 0, 2, 0, 10
2000 END
```

Group 4 and General Programs

There are quite a few programs to choose from here. Enough that you should probably take at least two sessions at the computer to pick some that you like, type them in, debug your mistakes, and then try some changes. Just beware of overload.

A NESTED LOOP

```
10 FOR X=1 TO 10
20 FOR Y=1 TO 5
30 PRINT X;"*";Y"="X*Y
40 NEXT Y
50 NEXT X
60 END
```

TRY TURNING THIS INTO
A QUIZ USING INPUT

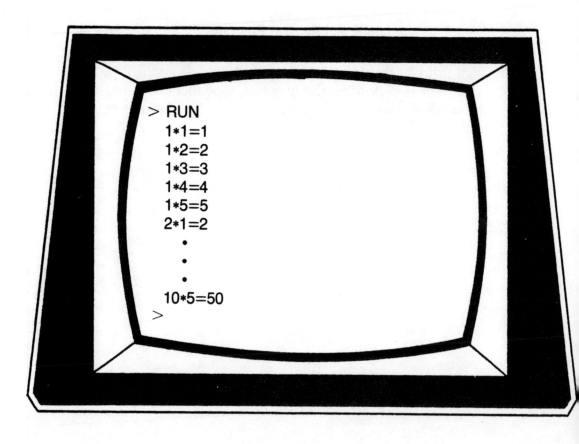

```
> RUN
  1*1=1
  1*2=2
  1*3=3
  1*4=4
  1*5=5
  2*1=2
    •
    •
    •
  10*5=50
>
```

SELECTIVELY READING DATA
```
10 LET T=0
20 READ N:IF N=0 THEN END
30 FOR D=1 TO N
40 READ X
50 LET T=T+X
60 NEXT D
70 PRINT "TOTAL=";T
80 GOTO 10
90  DATA 3,15,15,15,4,1,10,10,10,5,
    25,25,25,25,10,6,1,30,50,60,80,90,0
```

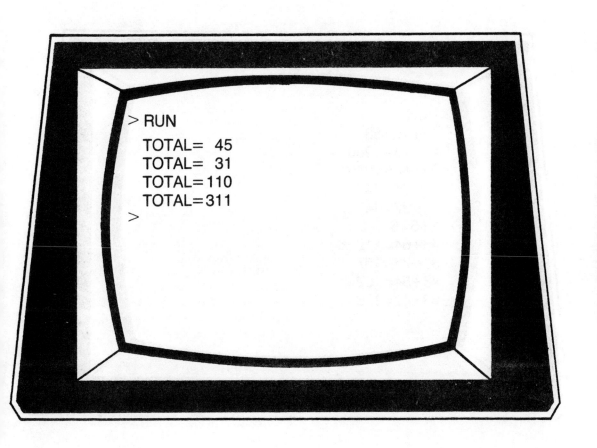

```
> RUN
  TOTAL=  45
  TOTAL=  31
  TOTAL=110
  TOTAL=311
>
```

```
10 PRINT "ADVANCED MATH"
30 FOR X=1 TO 10
40 READ A,B
50 C=A+B
60 PRINT A;"+";B"=";C
70 NEXT X
80 DATA 12,46,214,46,231,45,47,95,12,32
90 DATA 1,5,48,64,32,75,48,54,69,47
100 END
```

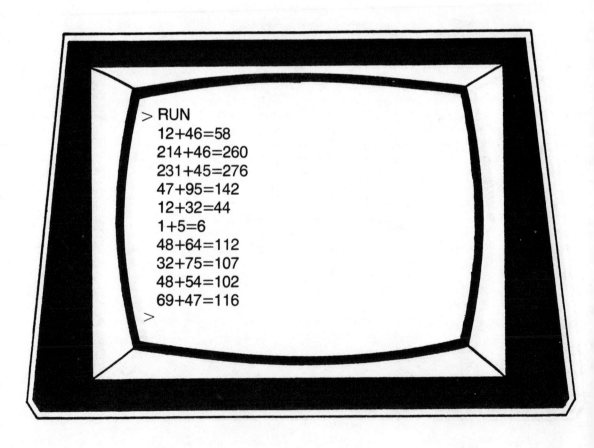

```
> RUN
  12+46=58
  214+46=260
  231+45=276
  47+95=142
  12+32=44
  1+5=6
  48+64=112
  32+75=107
  48+54=102
  69+47=116
>
```

```
10 PRINT "STRANGE NUMBERS"
20 X=0
30 Y=1
40 FOR Z=1 TO 20
50 PRINT X;
60 PRINT TAB(11)"+";
70 PRINT TAB(15)Y
80 X=X+Y
90 Y=X+Y
100 NEXT Z
```

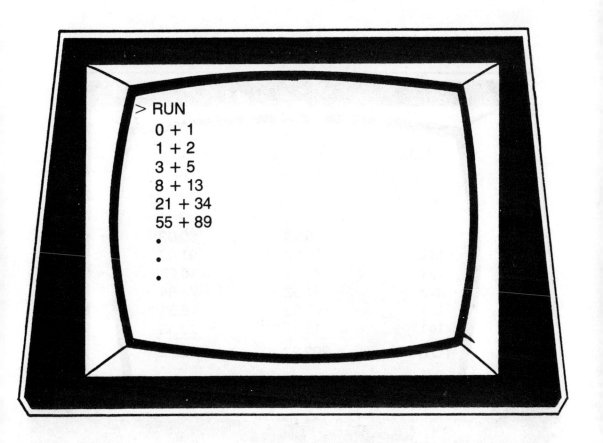

```
 10 PRINT "ACCOUNT #","DEBIT","CREDIT"
 20 READ A,B,C,D,E,F,G,H,I,J K,L
 30 DATA 10.23,50.09,73.84,91.02,20.53
 40 DATA 46.51,50.09,91.20,10.23,73.84
 50 DATA 46.51,20.53
 60 PRINT "111",A,G
 70 PRINT "112",B,H
 80 PRINT "121",C,I
 90 PRINT "012",D,J
100 PRINT "131",E,K
110 PRINT "141",F,L
120 PRINT "       "," _____ ", " _____ "
130 LET DB=A+B+C+D+E+F
140 LET CR=G+H+I+J+K+L
150 PRINT "TOTALS",DB,CR
```

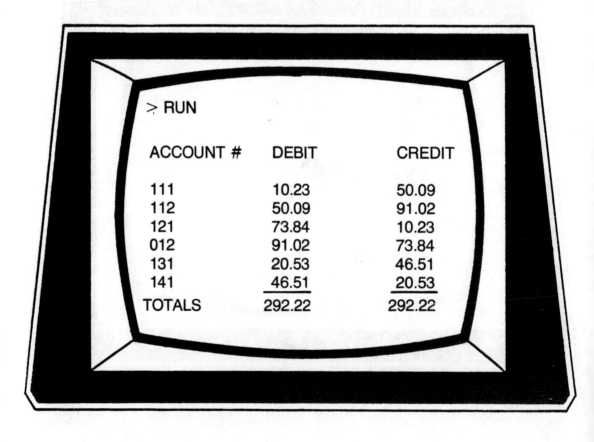

```
> RUN

ACCOUNT #        DEBIT          CREDIT

111              10.23          50.09
112              50.09          91.02
121              73.84          10.23
012              91.02          73.84
131              20.53          46.51
141              46.51          20.53
TOTALS          292.22         292.22
```

```
10 PRINT "TABULATION BY VARIABLES"
20 X=20
30 PRINT TAB(X-16)"START";TAB(X-8)"END";
     TAB(X)"MILES";TAB(X+8)"MPG"
40 READ A,B,C
50 PRINT TAB(X-16)A;TAB(X-8)B;TAB(X)B-A;TAB(X+8)INT(B-A)/C
60 GOTO 40
70 DATA 21423,21493,5,15270,15504,13
```

> BY ADJUSTING X IN LINE 20
> YOU CAN DISPLAY THE BLOCK
> ANYWHERE YOU WANT ON
> THE SCREEN.

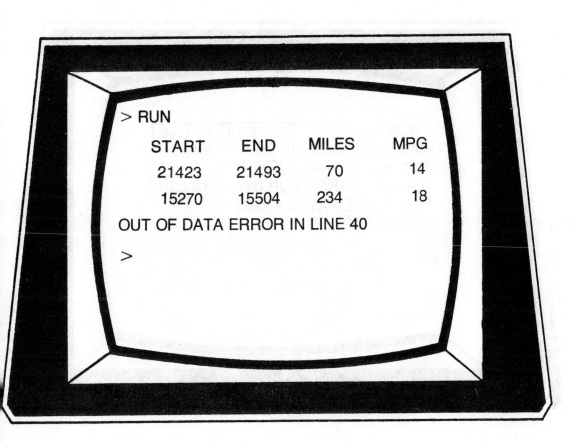

```
> RUN
      START      END     MILES      MPG
      21423    21493       70        14
      15270    15504      234        18
OUT OF DATA ERROR IN LINE 40

>
```

```
 50  PRINT "WAGES EARNED"
 60  INPUT W
 70  IF W=0 THEN STOP  ◀——— THE GOTO IN LINE 190 WOULD REPEAT
                             INDEFINITELY WITHOUT THIS LINE.
 80  IF W< 118 THEN TAX=0:GOTO 160
 90  IF W< 275 THEN TAX=((W−118)*.15:GOTO 160
100  IF W< 567 THEN TAX=((W−275)*.18)+23.55:GOTO 160
110  IF W< 850 THEN TAX=((W−567)*.21)+76.11:GOTO 160
120  IF W< 1183 THEN TAX=((W−850)*.26)+135.54:GOTO 160
130  IF W × 1433 THEN TAX=((W−1183)*.30)+222.12:GOTO 160
140  IF W< 1875 THEN TAX=((W−1433)*.34)+297.12:GOTO 160
150  IF W> 1875 THEN TAX=((W−1875)*.39)+441.40
160  PRINT "YOU GOT TAKEN FOR";TAX;"DOLLARS."
170  PRINT "TAKE HOME PAY IS" W−TAX
180  PRINT:PRINT
190  GOTO 50
```

```
> RUN
WAGES EARNED      NOTE DON'T USE
?500  ◀———        DOLLAR SIGN OR
                  COMMAS.
YOU GOT TAKEN FOR 64.05 DOLLARS.
TAKE HOME PAY IS 435.95
WAGES EARNED
?0
>
```

Here is a way to stop a GOTO loop when reading from DATA statements.

```
10  PRINT "COUNTING VOTES"
20  N=0:X=0:Y=0:Z=0
30  DATA 2,4,3,1,3,1,3,4,2,1,3,1,4,1,2,4,9999
60  READ A
70  IF A=9999 THEN GOTO 210
80  IF A<> 1 THEN GOTO 90
85  N=N+1
90  IF A<> 2 THEN GOTO 100
95  X=X+1
100 IF A<> 3 THEN GOTO 110
105 Y=Y+1
110 IF A<> 4 THEN GOTO 60 ◄──┤ IF A ISN'T 1-4 THEN IT ISN'T COUNTED.
115 Z=Z+1
120 GOTO 60
210 PRINT TAB(15)N, "ONES"
215 PRINT TAB(15)X, "TWOS"
220 PRINT TAB(15)Y, "THREES"
225 PRINT TAB(15)Z, "FOURS"
230 END
```

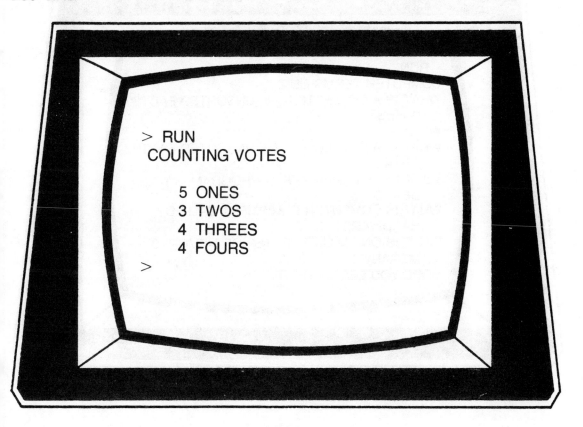

```
> RUN
COUNTING VOTES

     5 ONES
     3 TWOS
     4 THREES
     4 FOURS
>
```

YOU CAN ADD
REWARDS FOR
PROPER ANSWERS

```
 10 PRINT "COMPUTER TERMS QUIZ"
 20 INPUT "WHAT IS A COLLECTION OF UNSORTED FACTS";AN$
 40 IF AN$= "DATA" THEN GOTO 60
 50 PRINT "WRONG":GOTO 20
 60 INPUT "TO CORRECT ERRORS IN A PROGRAM IS TO___ ";AN$
 80 IF AN$="DEBUG" THEN GOTO 100
 90 PRINT "WRONG": GOTO 60
100 INPUT "WHAT IS COMPUTER EQUIPMENT CALLED";AN$
110 IF AN$="HARDWARE" THEN GOTO 120
110 PRINT "WRONG":GOTO 100
120 INPUT "WHAT IS ONE MILLION BYTES OF MEMORY";AN$
130 IF AN$="MEGABYTE" THEN GOTO 150
140 PRINT "WRONG":GOTO 120
150 PRINT "HOPE YOU LEARNED SOMETHING!"
160 END
```

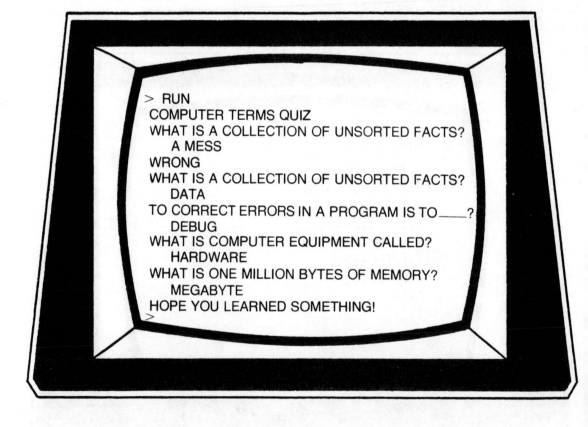

```
> RUN
COMPUTER TERMS QUIZ
WHAT IS A COLLECTION OF UNSORTED FACTS?
    A MESS
WRONG
WHAT IS A COLLECTION OF UNSORTED FACTS?
    DATA
TO CORRECT ERRORS IN A PROGRAM IS TO____?
    DEBUG
WHAT IS COMPUTER EQUIPMENT CALLED?
    HARDWARE
WHAT IS ONE MILLION BYTES OF MEMORY?
    MEGABYTE
HOPE YOU LEARNED SOMETHING!
>
```

Besides being those funny little characters you can draw pictures with, graphics are also normal characters used in any unusual way. If they move, for instance.

```
10 FOR I=1 TO 20
20 CLS
30 PRINT TAB(I) "COME"
40 PRINT TAB(40-1)"TOGETHER"
50 FOR J=1 TO 50
60 NEXT J
70 NEXT I
80 GOTO 80
```

THIS LINE KEEPS THE SCREEN FROM BEING DISTURBED AT THE END OF THE PROGRAM. USE BREAK TO STOP IT.

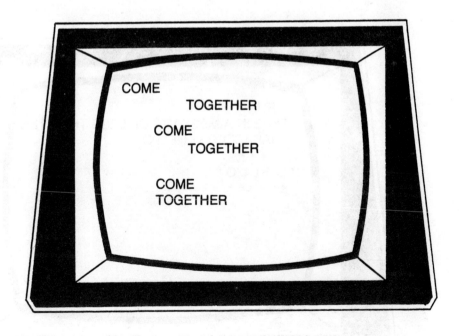

```
10  INPUT "TYPE IN A MESSAGE OF LESS THAN TEN CHARACTERS";A$
20  B$=" * * * * * *"
30  C$="* * * * * * *"
40  CLS
50  FOR I=1 TO 10:PRINT:NEXT I
55  FOR I=1 TO 500
60  IF I=INT(I/2)*2 THEN GOTO 110   ◄─── I=INT(I/2)*2 IS ONLY TRUE WHEN I IS EVEN
70  PRINT TAB(20)B$
80  PRINT TAB(20)"*";A$;TAB(33)"*"
90  PRINT TAB(20)B$
100 NEXT I:END                      ◄─── NOTICE TWO NEXTS FOR ONE FOR.
110 PRINT TAB(20)C$                       IF YOUR COMPUTER WON'T DO
120 PRINT TAB(20)" ";A$;TAB(33)" "         THIS CHANGE 100 TO GOTO 140.
130 PRINT TAB(20)C$                        SOME BASICS WILL DO THIS OK
140 NEXT I:END                      ◄─── BUT WON'T COMPILE RIGHT. (See Chap. 3)
```

Suppose you have a decimal number such as 123.4567 and you want to chop off all but one decimal place. INT chops off the decimals, but you want to save that 4 also. Multiplying by ten will move the decimal over so the number is 1234.567, 123.4! The BASIC code looks like this:

```
A=123.4567
A=INT(A*10)/10
PRINT A
```

Now, suppose instead of just chopping the excess decimal off, you want to round it to one decimal place? First multiply to get to the last decimal you want. Here we would multiply by ten to get 1234.567. If the first number after the decimal is 5 or above we want to round up, if it is below 5 we round down. You could do this with an IF . . . THEN, but that would be too messy. If we just add .5 the same effect will be achieved. Then we INT and divide by ten, just like above.

```
A=123.4567
A=INT(A*10+.5)/10
PRINT A
```

Dollars and cents is written in two decimal places. Five dollars and twenty five cents is 5. 25, for example. To round to two places use 100 for multiplying and dividing. For three decimal places use 1000.

Try these examples before doing the next program.

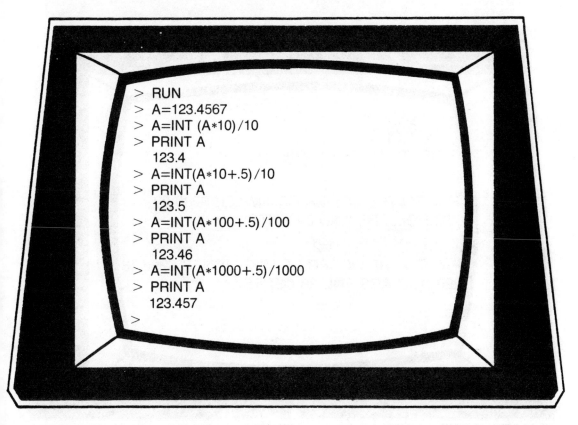

```
> RUN
> A=123.4567
> A=INT (A*10)/10
> PRINT A
  123.4
> A=INT(A*10+.5)/10
> PRINT A
  123.5
> A=INT(A*100+.5)/100
> PRINT A
  123.46
> A=INT(A*1000+.5)/1000
> PRINT A
  123.457
>
```

```
 10  PRINT "PAYROLL"
 20  INPUT "FIRST CHECK NUMBER";N
 30  READ E
 40  FOR I=1 TO E
 50  READ P$,H,R
 60  M=H*R:V=0
 70  IF H< =40 THEN GOTO 105
 80  V=H−40
 90  V=V+V/2
100  M=M+V*R
105  M=INT(M*100+.5)/100
110  FOR J=1 TO 6:PRINT:NEXT J
120  PRINT TAB(50)"#";N+E−1
130  PRINT "PAY TO THE ORDER OF";P$;TAB(45)"$";M
140  PRINT TAB(21)INT(M);"DOLLARS AND";M−INT(M);"CENTS"
150  FOR J=1 TO 6:PRINT:NEXT J
160  NEXT I
1000  DATA 2
1010  DATA JIM LEE,40,7,MIKE JONES,45,6.25
```

```
>  RUN
   PAYROLL
   FIRST CHECK NUMBER;1

            #1
   PAY TO THE ORDER OF JIM LEE $280.00
   280 DOLLARS AND 0 CENTS

            #2
   PAY TO THE ORDER OF MIKE JONES $296.88
   296 DOLLARS AND 88 CENTS


>
```

There are times when you will want to branch only if two different variables are meeting certain conditions. For example branch if A is 5 and B is 4. You could do this with two IF statements like this.

10 IF A < > 5 THEN GOTO 200
20 IF B < > THEN GOTO 200
100 Condition met code

•

•

200 Condition not met code

•

•

There is a way to combine these two IFs into one statement. Remember that when you compare two items the computer replaces the comparison with a zero if it is not true and a one if it is true. These values can be added and multiplied just like any other numbers. The IF looks at the result, and if it is zero does not branch. If it is greater than zero it branches. This means we can combine the IFs like this.

IF (A < > 5) + (B < > 4) THEN GOTO 200
If either of those statements is true or both of them are true then the branch is made. Only if they are both untrue (which means A=5 and B=4) does BASIC go to the next line.

What if our blocks of code were reversed? We only want to jump to 200 if both A=5 and B=4. That could be written like this.

IF (A=5) * (B=4) THEN GOTO 200
Zero times anything is zero, so if either one, or both of the comparisons are not true the result is zero and the branch isn't made.

The next program uses this concept.

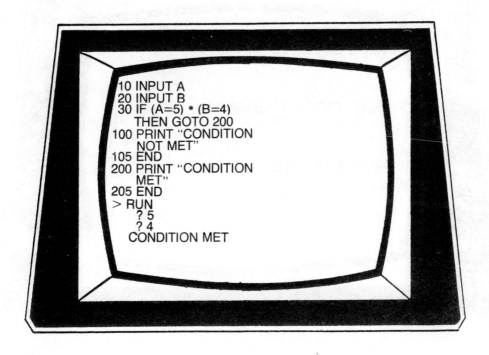

```
10 INPUT A
20 INPUT B
30 IF (A=5) * (B=4)
   THEN GOTO 200
100 PRINT "CONDITION
    NOT MET"
105 END
200 PRINT "CONDITION
    MET"
205 END
> RUN
  ? 5
  ? 4
  CONDITION MET
```

This program introduces another new concept. You can usually put any command on an IF. . .THEN statement. If you can't on your computer, make a block of code after the GOTO 20 statement. Alternate print statements for each of the strings with GOTO 140 statements, then branch to the proper one from lines 70-130.

```
   5 A$=". . . . ."
   6 B$=". *  ."
   7 C$=".  *  ."
   8 D$=".   *."
   9 E$=". * *."
  10 F$=".      ."
  20 INPUT "PRESS ENTER TO START";D$
  30 A=INT(6*RND(0))+1
  40 CLS
  50 PRINT A$
  60 FOR I=1 TO 3
  70 IF ((A=2)+(A=3))*(I=1) THEN PRINT B$
  80 IF ((A=2)+(A=3))*(I=3) THEN PRINT D$
  90 IF ((A=1)+(A=3) + (A=5)*(I=2) THEN PRINT C$
 100 IF (A>3)*((I=1)+(I=3)) THEN PRINT E$
 110 IF (A=6)*(I=2) THEN PRINT E$
 120 IF ((A=2) + (A=4)*(I=2) THEN PRINT F$
 130 IF (A=1)*((I=1)+(I=3)) THEN PRINT F$
 140 NEXT I:PRINT A$
 150 GOTO 20
```

```
ALTERNATE METHOD:
 . . . GOTO 200
 . . . GOTO 220
     200 PRINT B$
     210 GOTO 140
     220 PRINT D$
     230 GOTO 140
```

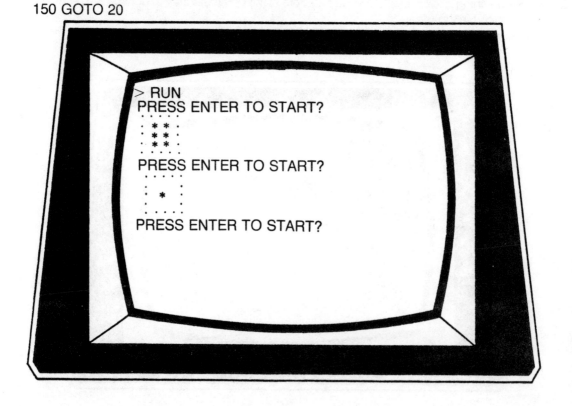

```
10 PRINT "CHANGE MAKER"
20 INPUT "COST OF ITEM ";A
30 INPUT "MONEY GIVEN ";B
40 IF B< A THEN GOTO 250
50 IF A=B THEN GOTO 240
60 C=B−A:PRINT"CHANGE IS $";C;" TO BE GIVEN AS FOLLOWS"
70 READ Z,T$
80 E=C/Z
90 IF E< 1 THEN GOTO 70
100 G=INT(E)
110 PRINT G,T$
120 C=C−(G*Z)
130 IF C=0 THEN END
140 GOTO 70
150 DATA 20, TWENTIES, 10, TENS, 5, FIVES, 1, ONES,. 25 QUARTERS
160 DATA .10, DIMES, .05, NICKELS, .01, PENNIES
240 PRINT "NO CHANGE NEEDED. ":END
250 PRINT "NOT ENOUGH MONEY":GOTO 30
```

Line 80 annotation: CHECKS TO SEE IF DENOMINATION IS PART OF CHANGE.

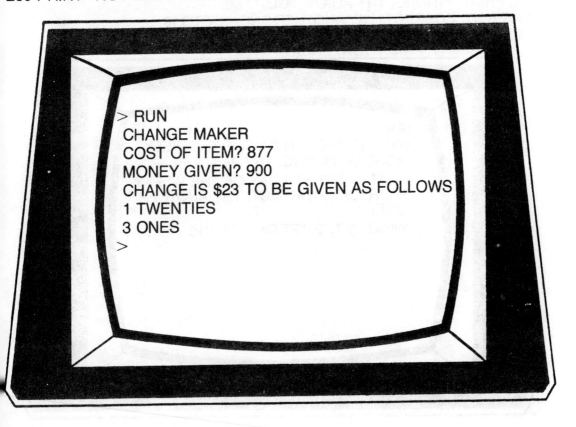

```
> RUN
CHANGE MAKER
COST OF ITEM? 877
MONEY GIVEN? 900
CHANGE IS $23 TO BE GIVEN AS FOLLOWS
1 TWENTIES
3 ONES
>
```

The last program read down a list of DATA one at a time. The data was organized so that each needed to be used only once. There may be times, however, when you will want to read the data list over and over. If you are reading each item from a FOR/NEXT loop at whatever point you stop the loop, the last item read will be the one that is remembered. This little program illustrates the technique.

```
10 A=INT(7*RND(0))+1
20 IF A=1 THEN A$="ST"
30 IF A=2 THEN A$="ND"
40 IF A=3 THEN A$="RD"
50 IF A>3 THEN A$ = "TH"
55 RESTORE
60 PRINT "WHAT IS THE ";A;A$;" DAY OF THE WEEK";
70 INPUT B$
80 FOR I=1 TO A
90 READ C$
100 NEXT I
110 IF C$=B$ THEN GOTO 130
120 PRINT "WRONG. TRY AGAIN." 'GOTO 60
130 PRINT "CORRECT! TRY ANOTHER ONE." :GOTO 10
140 DATA SUNDAY, MONDAY, TUESDAY, WEDNESDAY,
      THURSDAY, FRIDAY, SATURDAY
```

> REMEMBER ANY STATEMENT CAN BE USED AFTER AN IF . . . THEN ON MOST COMPUTERS.

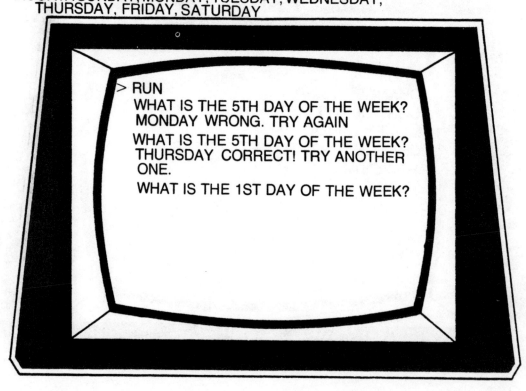

```
> RUN
  WHAT IS THE 5TH DAY OF THE WEEK?
  MONDAY WRONG. TRY AGAIN

  WHAT IS THE 5TH DAY OF THE WEEK?
  THURSDAY CORRECT! TRY ANOTHER
  ONE.

  WHAT IS THE 1ST DAY OF THE WEEK?
```

You can use two separate, distinct groups of data as long as you know how many items are in each group. In the menu below we are trying to make random meat and vegetable meals. We want the selection from each group to be random, and we want to use it for seven meals. After counting through the first list a random distance and taking our selection, we want the next loop to completely finish going through the list before counting out the random number for the second group. To do this we take the size of the first group and subtract from it how far into that group we counted. This number is the number of items left in the first group. If we add that number to the random number for the second group we solve the problem.

```
10 FOR I=1 TO 7
20 M=INT (5*RND(0))+1    ◄── RANDOM DISTANCE INTO FIRST GROUP
30 V=INT (7*RND(0))+1    ◄── RANDOM DISTANCE INTO SECOND GROUP
40 FOR J=1 TO M
50 READ M$
60 NEXT J
70 FOR J=1 TO V+5−M    ◄── 5 ITEMS—RANDOM DISTANCE INTO LIST
                            ADDED TO 2ND LIST RANDOM NUMBER.
80 READ V$
90 NEXT J
100 PRINT "DAY";I;"MENU ";M$;"−";V$
110 RESTORE
120 NEXT I
130 DATA CHICKEN, ROAST BEEF, LAMB, PORK CHOPS,
    HAMBURGERS
140 DATA GREEN BEANS, TOMATOES, CORN, BEETS, PEAS, SQUASH,
    BROCCOLI
150 END
```

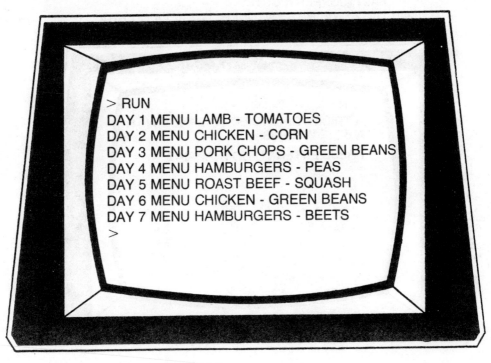

```
> RUN
DAY 1 MENU LAMB - TOMATOES
DAY 2 MENU CHICKEN - CORN
DAY 3 MENU PORK CHOPS - GREEN BEANS
DAY 4 MENU HAMBURGERS - PEAS
DAY 5 MENU ROAST BEEF - SQUASH
DAY 6 MENU CHICKEN - GREEN BEANS
DAY 7 MENU HAMBURGERS - BEETS
>
```

Here is another example using four lists of data.

```
10 A=INT (8*RND(0))+1
20 B=INT (8*RND(0))+1
30 C=INT (8*RND(0))+1
40 D=INT (8*RND(0))+1
50 RESTORE
60 FOR I=1 TO A
70 READ A$
80 NEXT I
90 FOR I=1 TO B+8-A
100 READ B$
110 NEXT I
120 FOR I=1 TO C+8-B
130 READ C$
140 NEXT I
150 FOR I=1 TO D+8-C
160 READ D$
170 NEXT I
180 PRINT "A ";A$;" GIRL TRIED TO ";B$;" WITH A ";C$;" ";D$
190 INPUT "PRESS ENTER TO DO AGAIN";DU$
```

INPUT USES THIS, BUT NOTHING ELSE DOES:
IT IS CALLED A DUMMY VARIABLE.

```
200 GOTO 10
210 DATA BRIGHT, SHY, SLY, TRICKY, SKINNY, BAGGY,
    COLD, BITTER
220 DATA DANCE, SING, ELOPE, TRAIN, SWING, FIGHT,
    ARGUE, TEASE
230 DATA RED, BLUE, CHEERY, GRUMPY, SHORT,
    FAST, SLIPPERY, CUTE
240 DATA WALRUS, NOODLE, GORILLA, ZEBRA,
    SPIDER, SNAKE, TURTLE, GNAT
```

> RUN

A TRICKY GIRL TRIED TO DANCE WITH
A BLUE WALRUS.

PRESS ENTER TO DO IT AGAIN?

The number of nested loops you can have depends on your computer. Most will allow as many as you have memory for but its hard to tell in advance because as you add loops the program grows, and as the program grows available memory decreases.

In the next chapter you will study subscripted variables. Perhaps then you will understand why you might need three or more loops nested in a program, for now just try this program and see if you can learn binary.

```
10 FOR A=0 TO 1
20 FOR B=0 TO 1
30 FOR C=0 TO 1
40 FOR D=0 TO 1
50 FOR E=0 TO 1
60 FOR F=0 TO 1
70 FOR G=0 TO 1
80 FOR H=0 TO 1
90 PRINT A;B;C;D;E;F;G;H; " = ";128*A+64*B+32*C+16*D+8*E+4*F+2*G+H
100 NEXT H, G, F, E, D  C, B, A
110 INPUT "PRESS ENTER TO DO AGAIN";A$
```

You could even add a ninth loop after the print statement to delay.

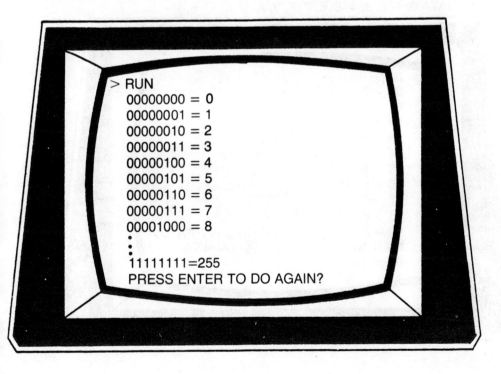

```
> RUN
  00000000 = 0
  00000001 = 1
  00000010 = 2
  00000011 = 3
  00000100 = 4
  00000101 = 5
  00000110 = 6
  00000111 = 7
  00001000 = 8
  :
  :
  11111111=255
  PRESS ENTER TO DO AGAIN?
```

When a programmer directly addresses his (or her) instructions to the chip, instead of to the BASIC interpreter (which is what you do when you write a program in BASIC) it is called writing machine language. As you just saw, it is hard to read all those ones and zeroes, so these people use a counting system based on sixteen digits called hexadecimal. After 9, instead of making up new digits, they use the letters A through F to represent numbers so you count 0, 1, 2, 3, 4, 5, 6, 7, 8, 9, A, B, C, D, E, F, 10, 11, 12, 13, 14, 15, 16, 17, 18, 19, 1A, 1B, 1C, 1D, 1E, 1F, 20, . . . They do this because each byte of memory can then be represented by two hex digits. Here is a program that uses FOR / NEXT, DATA, and strings to count in hex from 0 to FF.

```
10 FOR I=0 TO 255
20 A=INT(I / 16)
30 B=I−A*16
40 RESTORE
50 FOR J=0 TO A
60 READ A$
70 NEXT J
80 RESTORE
90 FOR J=0 TO B
100 READ B$
110 NEXT J
120 PRINT I;" = ";A$;B$; "IN HEX"
130 NEXT I
140 INPUT "PRESS ENTER TO DO AGAIN";D$:GOTO 10
150 DATA 0, 1, 2, 3, 4, 5, 6, 7, 8, 9, A, B, C, D, E, F
```

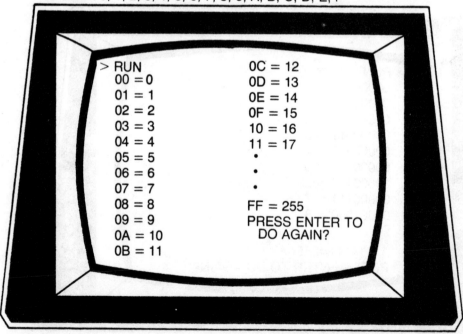

```
> RUN                    0C = 12
  00 = 0                 0D = 13
  01 = 1                 0E = 14
  02 = 2                 0F = 15
  03 = 3                 10 = 16
  04 = 4                 11 = 17
  05 = 5
  06 = 6                  .
  07 = 7
  08 = 8                  .
  09 = 9                 FF = 255
  0A = 10                PRESS ENTER TO
  0B = 11                   DO AGAIN?
```

In an effort to simplify binary without using special digits, computer people come up with a base 8 system called octal. The 8 bits in a byte are broken into groups of 3, with the highest group having only 2 bits. Each group can represent 8

1 byte	bit 7	bit 6	bit 5	bit 4	bit 3	bit 2	bit 1	bit 0

group 3　　　group 2　　　group 1

digits from 0 to 7, the last group represents 4 digits from 0 to 3. The instructions to many chips are derived from octal groupings, so here is a program to teach counting in octal.

```
10 FOR I=0 TO 3
20 FOR J=0 TO 7
30 FOR K=0 TO 7
40 PRINT I;J;K; "EQUALS";I*64+J*8+K
50 NEXT K,J,I
60 GOTO 10
```

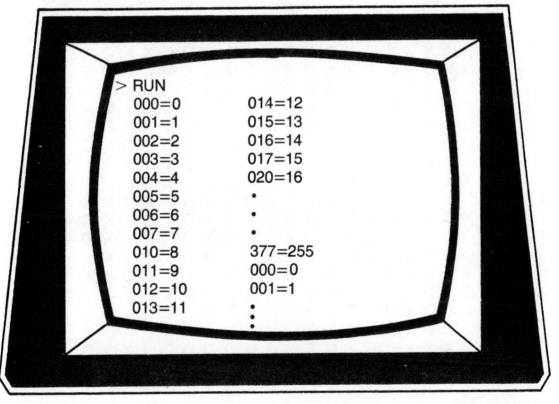

```
> RUN
000=0        014=12
001=1        015=13
002=2        016=14
003=3        017=15
004=4        020=16
005=5          •
006=6          •
007=7          •
010=8
011=9        377=255
012=10       000=0
013=11       001=1
               •
               •
               •
```

The computer prints up a playing field. The object is to connect any two corners of the square with the fewest possible Xs, using only Xs for your path. Don't stop just because you've managed to connect two corners. There may be a shorter path between two different corners.

```
10 FOR X=1 TO 20
20 FOR Y=1 TO 20
30 IF ((X=1) + (X=20))*((Y=1)+(Y=20))  THEN
PRINT"X";:GOTO 70
40 Z=INT (2*RND(0))+1
50 IF Z=1 THEN PRINT "X";
60 IF Z=2 THEN PRINT "O";
70 NEXT Y
80 PRINT
90 NEXT X
100 GOTO 100
```

PRINT AN X IN EACH CORNER

SEMICOLON KEEPS PRINTING
ON SAME LINE

NEEDED TO START PRINTING
ON NEW LINE.

KEEPS SCREEN FROM SCROLLING.
USE BREAK TO END.

```
> RUN
X O X X X O O O X O X X X O O O X X O X
O X O O O X X X O X O X O X X O X O O O
X X O O X X X X X O O X O O O O O X X O
X X O X O O X O O O O O X O O O O X O X
O X O X O O X X X O O X O O O X X X O X
O X O X O O X X X O O O X X X O O O X O
X X O X O O X X O O O X O O O X X X X X
X X X X O O O O X O X X O O X O O O O O
O O O X O X O O X O O O X X O X X X X X
X O X O O X O O X O O X O X O X O X X O
O O O X O O O X X X O X O X O X O O X O
O O X O O X O O O X X X O O O X O O X O
X X O O O O X O O X X X O O X O O O O X
O X O O X O X O X X X O O O O X O X O X
X O O X O X O O X O O X O X O O X O X X
O O O X O X O X X O X O O X O X O X O O
X X X X O O X O O O X O O O O O O X O O
X X X X O O O O O O O O O X X O X O X X
X O O O X X O X O O O X O X X O O X O X
```

If you hang around old computerists you may hear the term "benchmarking" used. What they are talking about is testing to see how fast the computer can do something. The computer can do each of its instructions so fast that you would never be able to time just one, but using a loop you can do a hundred or a thousand of the same instruction over and over and time the whole thing. First you have to time the loop itself. Try these three tests.

10 FOR A=1 TO 1000	10 A=1:B=1000	10 A=1:B=1000
20 NEXT A	20 FOR C=A TO B	20 FOR C=ATOB:
	30 NEXT C	NEXTC

Time each loop with a second hand or stop watch. You should notice quite a difference. Now, insert a single command inside the loop, such as D= or PRINT. Each command takes a different amount of time. When you are writing long programs it is good to know which commands work the fastest.

You can use your computer to keep notes, as shown below. You will use these notes in the next example.

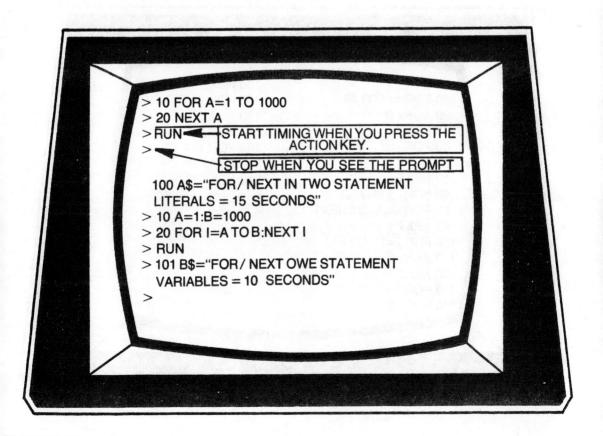

139

Even if your computer wasn't meant to play music, you can coax some out of it. Use the figures from the last experiment to calculate how many of each instruction are done each second. For instance, if a loop of 1000 print statements takes 15 seconds then the computer does 66⅔ prints per second.

Try to find two commands that meet these rules:
1.) One is exactly double the other.
2.) There are 6 other commands with times between them.

The first two commands define the octave. Define their difference by 12. Use the successive differences to calculate notes in the octave. Example:

55	59½	64	68½	73	77½	82	86½	91	95½	100	104½	110
FOR / NEXT	A / 5		A / B		A+1	A+B				GOTO	REM	DATA

It won't come out exactly equal. Try to get close. Now, write a series of loops to play your song. To hear it, turn on a radio. Tune to about 850 on AM or 1400 on FM. There will be some place near the computer that you will be able to set the radio and hear the music.

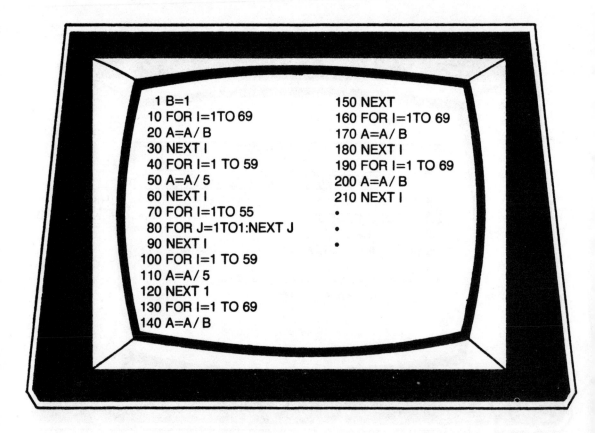

```
1 B=1
10 FOR I=1TO 69
20 A=A/ B
30 NEXT I
40 FOR I=1 TO 59
50 A=A/ 5
60 NEXT I
70 FOR I=1TO 55
80 FOR J=1TO1:NEXT J
90 NEXT I
100 FOR I=1 TO 59
110 A=A/ 5
120 NEXT 1
130 FOR I=1 TO 69
140 A=A/ B

150 NEXT
160 FOR I=1TO 69
170 A=A/ B
180 NEXT I
190 FOR I=1 TO 69
200 A=A/ B
210 NEXT I
 •
 •
 •
```

There are two ways to do graphics using the basic powers we have learned.

The first is with the print statement. Each line of the figure is a string.

```
10 A$="     XX      "
20 B$="    XXXX     "
30 C$=" XXXXXXXX "
40 D$="    O O     "
50 PRINT A$:PRINT B$: PRINT C$:PRINT D$
```

The second is with the data statement in a loop. It saves some space.

```
10 FOR I=1 TO 4
20 READ A$:PRINT A$:NEXT I
30 DATA "     XX      "
40 DATA "    XXXX     "
50 DATA " XXXXXXXX "
60 DATA "    O O     "
```

Position on the screen can be controlled by a print loop before the character is printed, and tabs in the print statements.

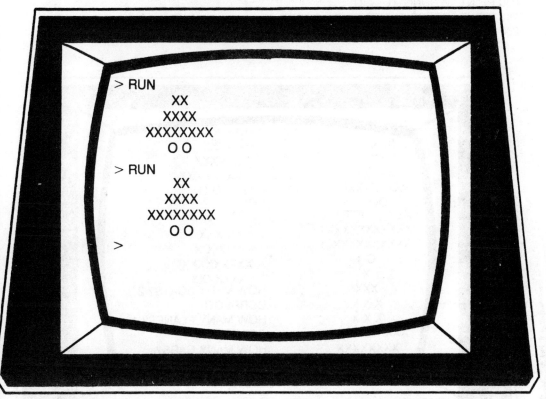

DATA GRAPHICS

```
10 B=0 D=0 : CLS
20 FOR I=1TO5
30 X=INT (3*RND(0)) +1
40 RESTORE
50 FOR Y=1 TO 4
60 READ A$:IF X=1 THEN PRINT A$
70 NEXT Y:FOR Y=1 TO 4
80 READ A$:IF X=2 THEN PRINT A$
90 NEXT Y:FOR Y=1 TO 6
100 READ A$:IF X=3 THEN PRINT A$
110 NEXT Y:IF X=1 THEN C=C+1
120 IF X=2 THEN P=P+1
130 IF X=3 THEN B=B+1
140 NEXT I
150 INPUT "HOW MANY BOATS?";A
160 IF A=B PRINT "CORRECT!":GOTO 180
170 PRINT "WRONG. IT IS";B
180 INPUT "HOW MANY PLANES?";0
190 IF P=Q THEN PRINT "CORRECT":GOTO 210
200 PRINT "WRONG. IT IS";P
210 INPUT "HOW MANY CARS";D
220 IF C=D THEN PRINT "CORRECT!": GOTO 240
230 PRINT "WRONG. IT IS";C
240 INPUT "PRESS ENTER TO DO AGAIN" A$
250 GOTO 10

500 DATA " XX              "
510 DATA "   XXXX          "
520 DATA " XXXXXXXX        "
530 DATA "    OO           "
540 DATA " XX        TTT  1 "
550 DATA " XXXXXXXXXXX     "
560 DATA " XXXXXXXXXX  1   "
570 DATA "         O   1   "
580 DATA "         X       "
590 DATA "        XXX      "
600 DATA "       X X X     "
610 DATA "       X X X     "
620 DATA " XXXXXXXXXXX     "
630 DATA "   XXXXXXXX      "
640 END
```

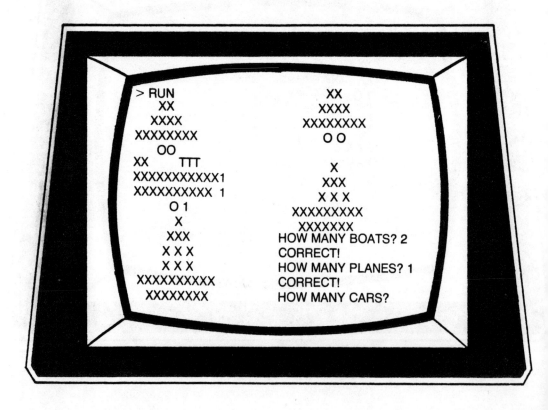

142

```
PRINT GRAPHICS
10 A$=" . . . . . . "
20 B$=" .          . "
30 C$=" . O  O . "
40 D$=" .   O   . "
50 E$=" . - - - . "
60 F$  " . . . . . . "
70 G$="       . .       "
80 CLS
90 INPUT "WHO IS BURIED IN GRANT'S TOMB";Z$
100 IF Z$ = "GRANT" THEN GOTO 130
110 PRINT "WRONG, HUMAN!"
120 GOTO 90
130 PRINT   A$;PRINT B$:PRINT C$:  PRINT
      D$:PRINT E$:PRINT F$:PRINT G$
140 PRINT "PRETTY GOOD . . . FOR A HU-
      MAN.":CLS
150 INPUT "WHEN WAS THE WAR OF 1812";Z$
160 IF Z$="1812" THEN GOTO 180
170 PRINT "WRONG, HUMAN":GOTO 150
180 PRINT    A$:PRINT  B$:PRINT  C$:PRINT
      D$:PRINT E$:PRINT F$:PRINT G$
190 PRINT "WELL DONE, HUMAN?"
200 END
```

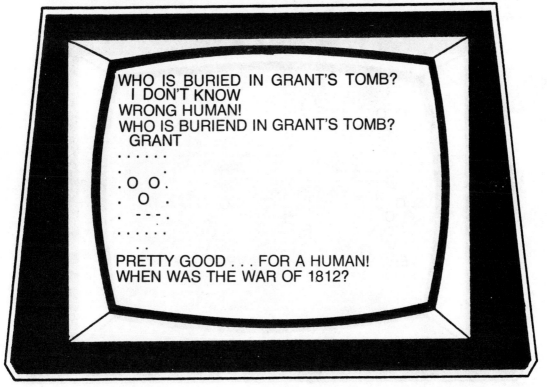

ANIMATION

You can animate the face of your creature by quickly switching what you draw.

Here is the correct answer routine.

```
10 A$=". . . . . . ."
20 B$=".         ."
30 C$=".   O O   ."
40 D$=".    O    ."
50 E$=".  - - -  ."
60 F$=". . . . . ."
70 G$="    . .    "
80 H$=". O O O ."
90 X$=" "
100 FOR I= 1 TO 6
110 CLS:IF I=INT(I / 2)*2 THEN GOTO 140
120 PRINT A$=PRINT B$=PRINT C$:PRINT D$:PRINT E$:PRINT F$:
    PRINT G$
130 PRINT X$:GOTO 160
140 PRINT A$:PRINT B$:PRINT C$:PRINT D$:PRINT H$:PRINT F$:PRINT G$
150 READ Z$: X$=X$+Z$: PRINT X$
160 NEXT I
170 DATA VERY, GOOD, HUMAN!
180 END
```

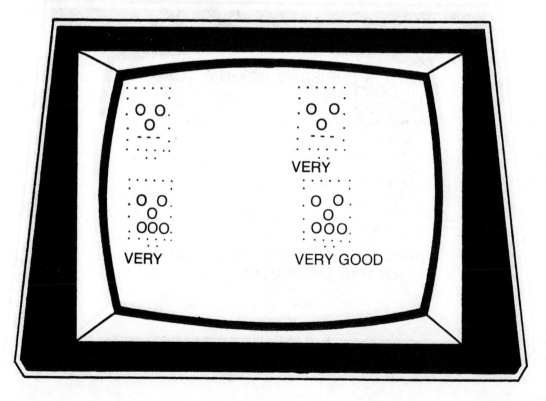

This program calculates the value of regular savings,
based on a given interest rate and monthly deposits.

```
10  T=0
20 INPUT "MONTHLY DEPOSIT";0
30 INPUT "HOW MANY YEARS ";Y
40 INPUT "YEARLY INTEREST RATE";I
50 FOR K=1 TO Y*12
60 T=T + (T*I / 12) / 100
70 T=T+0
80 NEXT K
90  PRINT "$";D;" DEPOSITED MONTHLY AT ";I;"%
    PER ANNUM FOR ";Y; "YEARS YIELDS $";T
100 END
```

SEE IF YOU CAN CHANGE THIS TO
ROUND THE ANSWER AND ALLOW
YOU TO DO ANOTHER PROBLEM.

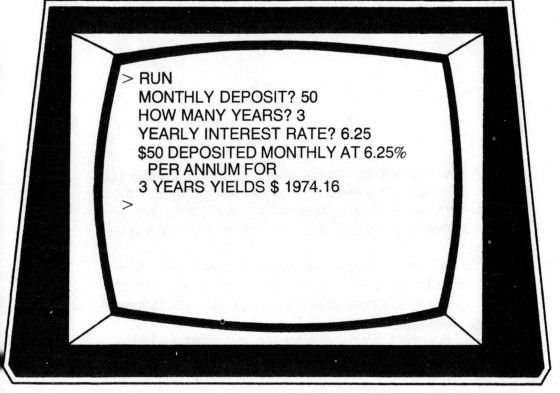

```
> RUN
MONTHLY DEPOSIT? 50
HOW MANY YEARS? 3
YEARLY INTEREST RATE? 6.25
$50 DEPOSITED MONTHLY AT 6.25%
 PER ANNUM FOR
3 YEARS YIELDS $ 1974.16
>
```

FLOWCHARTS

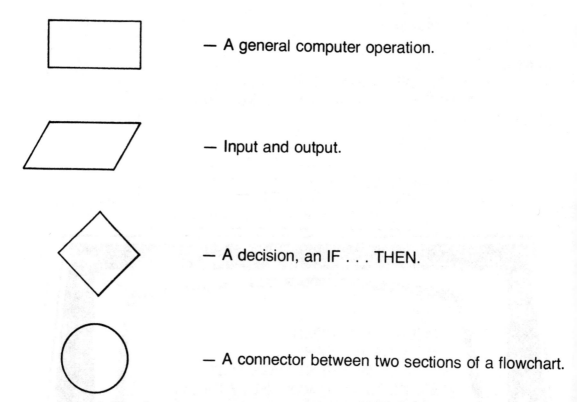

— A general computer operation.

— Input and output.

— A decision, an IF . . . THEN.

— A connector between two sections of a flowchart.

    A flowchart is a simple diagram that shows the flow of logic. There are many symbols, but you can get by with the four shown above. Professional programmers are required to keep flowcharts as part of the documentation of a program.

    You will find that developing your program with a flowchart will help you to keep from forgetting important steps and help you keep a clear idea of the steps you take to solve a programming problem.

    The flowchart opposite is for the last example in this chapter.

FLOWCHART FOR SECRET CODE

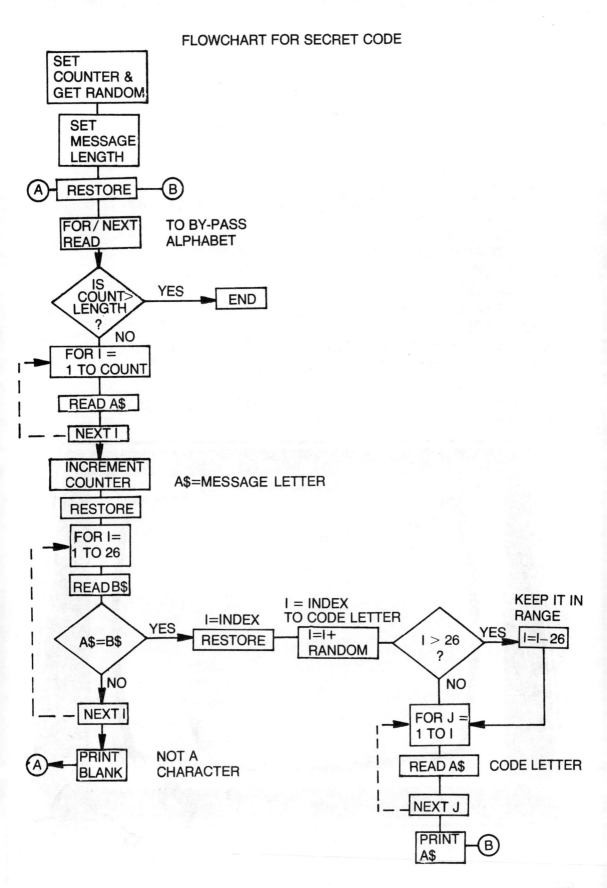

147

Type in a message, separating each letter with a comma, as DATA statement 1000, and this program will put it in secret code. Spaces must be in quotes. For example, DATA H,I, " ", T,H,E,R,E. The last thing on line 10 should be Y=# of characters.

```
10 Z=1:X=INT(26*RND(0))+1:Y=12
20 RESTORE:FOR I=1 TO 26:READ A$:NEXT I:IF Z>Y THEN END
30 FOR I=1 TO Z:READ A$:NEXT I
40 Z=Z+1
50 RESTORE:FOR I=1 TO 26
60 READ B$
70 IF A$=B$ THEN GOTO 90
80 NEXT I:PRINT " ";:GOTO 20
90 RESTORE
100 I=I+X: IF I>26 THEN I=I-26
110 FOR J=1 TO I:READ B$:NEXT J
120 PRINT B$;:GOTO 20
130 DATA A,B,C,D,E,F G,H,I,J K,L,M,N,O,P,Q,R,S,T,U,V,W,X,Y,Z
140 DATA Y,O,U,R, " ", M,E,S,S,A,G,E
```

```
> RUN
  ZPVS NFTTBHF
>
```

Chapter 6

More Power to Ya'!

Both types of variables are indeed like gypsies. They wander around in memory and take on different values from time to time. Like everything else, though, they have their uses. They allow us to write general routines and then plug in any value we want to use in that routine. If you want to use the routine again with a different number, just plug the number into the variable you used in the routine. Think about how miraculous the things you can already make the computer do are.

"Well," you might ask, "if I can use these magical powers to divide memory into little boxes and store things there, why can't I do something else? Like put little boxes into one giant box?"

You can. In several different ways, as a matter of fact. They are in a separate chapter because they vary so much from one computer to another. It would be hopeless to try to teach them along with the simple BASIC powers.

In almost every case you will have to consult with a teacher (they have their uses too) or the manual that came with your computer to get exact information about these ideas. Don't let that stop you from continuing, though. BASIC has a lot more secrets.

VARIABLES

The smallest division of memory that can be controlled from most BASICs is a byte. A byte can store a single character as a code known as ASCII. If the computer knows that it is supposed to read the byte as a character it decodes it into the correct one and puts it on the screen. If it knows that a character is to be stored in memory as a character, it encodes it to the proper value and stores it. If it doesn't know that the byte is a character, it can read it as a number. The largest number a byte can actually store is 255.

When we assign a variable, which is the same thing as naming a box and putting a value in it, the box is adjusted to the proper size by the computer so that it has only as many bytes in it as is necessary to hold what we put into it. A literal string that is one character long only requires one byte.

Numbers, unless they are stored as literal strings, will always require more than one byte. The computer has a special way that it can read two bytes together as one number. When it does this, it can represent whole numbers (integers) up to 65535. For this reason most small computers have 65535 as the upper limit for integers. An integer number takes up two bytes. To represent floating decimal point numbers requires at least three bytes, and more if you want better accuracy.

Most BASICs with floating point capabilities allow you to define whether a variable is to hold integers, single precision, or even double precision decimal numbers. You can make your boxes smaller, saving space, if you define all numbers that don't have to be floating point as integers.

STRINGS

Since each character in a string is one byte and BASIC can manipulate single bytes, why can't you manipulate single letters in a string? You can. Most BASICs have the ability to add two strings together to make one long one, and most have at least one power that can break a string down into smaller pieces.

The first BASIC had only two powers for strings. The first was SEGMENT and the second was &. SEGMENT had three arguments. The first was the string you were working with, the second was what character to start with, and the third was how many characters after that you wanted. If A$="I AM A COMPUTER" then B$=SEGMENT(A$, 5, 4) would start at the space (yes, space is a character) between AM and A and put four characters into B$. It would be the same as saying LET B$= "AC". The & simply added two strings together. If you said LET A$="HELLO "?"THERE" then A$ would contain "HELLO THERE".

As more versions of BASIC developed, people added other powers. Someone decided that it would be nice to know the length of the string so LEN was born. PRINT LEN("HELLO") would print 5. This is useful if you are using a FOR / NEXT loop to search through a string for a specific character. Some BASICs call it LENGTH.

When Microsoft started supplying BASIC to many of the small computer makers their's became the closest thing to a standard BASIC around. They decided to use the regular plus sign for adding strings, the word MID$ instead of SEGMENT, added LEFT$ and RIGHT$ and allowed you to compare strings with the same math symbols used for numbers.

LEFT$ and RIGHT$ are like special versions SEGMENT. LEFT$ always starts with the first character of the string, and takes as many characters as you tell it to. PRINT LEFT$("HELLO",3) would print HEL. RIGHT$ is not as easy to duplicate with SEGMENT. It starts with as many characters from the end as you tell it and takes all the rest up to the end. PRINT RIGHT$("HELLO",3) would print LLO.

The greater than, less than, and equals signs used for numbers can also be used for strings, except that they are compared alphabetically instead of numerically. "A" is greater than "B" and "BALL" is greater than "BALLOON". These symbols are great if you want the computer to alphabetize a list of titles or names.

STRING$ was also added. It makes a string as long as indicated, all from the same character, which is also indicated. PRINT STRING$("**", 6) would print ******.

Another item added to BASIC, specifically for strings, was the ability to change numbers into strings and strings into numbers. You know that you have to be careful not to mix these two up, but what if you have the number 125 and you want to store it somewhere as a string? If A=125, the LETB$ =STR$(A) is the same thing as LETB$="125". VAL does the reverse. A=VAL("34") equates A to 34 even though "34" is a literal string.

All of these commands work with literals and variables. Your computer may not have all of these, or they may not have the same name for the powers, but the concepts should be understood so you can use them when working on another computer, if you get that lucky.

There is one more set of powers used with strings that involves the ASCII code mentioned earlier. If you would like to see the ASCII code for a particular character type PRINT ASC(A$) where A$ is a single character string containing the character you want. If you know the ASCII code for a character you can turn the code into a single character string with CHR$.

Virtually every microcomputer has some variation of the ASCII code, and there is even some similarity in the format to use the code. On most microcomputers, the following program will display the code.

```
10 LET C=C+1
20 PRINT CHR$(C)
30 GOTO 10
```

You may want to put in a loop to slow down the display, but if you have the code in memory, this program should display it.

Numeric values concerned with numbers and upper case letters may be quite similar from one microcomputer to another, but lower case and graphic keys will vary wildly. The easiest way to use the code is to look it up in your computer manual. If you do not have a manual, you can use the powers printed above. A sample ASCII chart is shown on page 156.

ASCII CODE	CHARACTER	ASCII CODE	CHARACTER	ASCII CODE	CHARACTER
000	NULL	043	+	086	V
001	SOH	044	,	087	W
002	STX	045	–	088	X
003	ETX	046	.	089	Y
004	EOT	047	/	090	Z
005	ENQ	048	0	091	[
006	ACK	049	1	092	bkslash
007	BEL	050	2	093	]
008	BS	051	3	094	↑
009	HT	052	4	095	back arr
010	LF	053	5	096	space
011	VT	054	6	097	a
012	FF	055	7	098	b
013	CR	056	8	099	c
014	SO	057	9	100	d
015	SI	058	:	101	e
016	DLE	059	;	102	f
017	DC1	060	<	103	g
018	DC2	061	=	104	h
019	DC3	062	>	105	i
020	DC4	063	?	106	j
021	NAK	064	@	107	k
022	SYN	065	A	108	l
023	ETB	066	B	109	m
024	CAN	067	C	110	n
025	EM	068	D	111	o
026	SUB	069	E	112	p
027	ESCAPE	070	F	113	q
028	FS	071	G	114	r
029	GS	072	H	115	s
030	RS	073	I	116	t
031	US	074	J	117	u
032	SPACE	075	K	118	v
033	!	076	L	119	w
034	"	077	M	120	x
035	#	078	N	121	y
036	$	079	O	122	z
037	%	080	P	123	;
038	&	081	Q	124	<
039	'	082	R	125	=
040	(	083	S	126	>
041	)	084	T	127	DEL
042	*	085	U		

Most microcomputers use keyboard characters for some special function (usually in printing and spacing) both on the crt and on a printer. A common example is the PRINT power, which usually prints any material contained within two sets of quotation marks. When you want to print quotation marks within the PRINT power, BASIC may get confused and only print from the first set of quotation marks to the next set of quotation marks. To illustrate:

10 PRINT "THE GIRL SAID, "COME OVER." "

If this line were put into a microcomputer and RUN, many microcomputers would PRINT THE GIRL SAID, You can overcome this by changing the inside quotation marks into code values. As an example, let's say your code value for quotation marks is 34. The example line can be changed to:

10 PRINT "THE GIRL SAID, CHR$ (34) COME OVER. CHR$ (34)"

BASIC will obey the order to print character string 34, but will not recognize the character string to be quotation marks. This use, alone, is worth learning ASCII.

ARRAYS

Why can't you give one big box a name and store several numbers or strings in it? You can, but there is a small problem. Suppose you had twelve different colored marbles and you dump them into a shoe box. Now you want to get one specific colored marble out *without having to look through them to find that color*. Can't be done. What if you put them in an egg carton. It's a box. All you have to do is number, address, or index each cup in some way and then remember which cup each color is in. Since computers are perfect for addressing and remembering we have a perfect setup.

An array is a storage technique that allows you to put groups of information at indexed locations in memory so you can get parts of that information back in any sequence you wish at great speed. A *subscript* is a number used as an index (address) in the array, and a double subscript is simply two numbers used as an address in an array.

Let's start small. Here is an example of the world's smallest array.

10 LET A(1)=2
20 LET A(2)=3

Each subscript is a simple variable. You can have string arrays too! Single subscripted arrays can give you an idea of the power of arrays, so here is an example of one just to get you thinking about what an array looks like and feels like.

```
10 DIM A(12)
20 READ B
30 FOR C = 1 TO B
40 READ A
45 LET A(C) = A
50 NEXT C
60 FOR C = 1 TO B
70 PRINT A(C)
80 NEXT C
85 END
90 DATA 12
100 DATA 2,1,4,3,2,4,5,6,3,5,4,1
```

THE FIRST PIECE OF DATA TELLS HOW MANY MORE THERE ARE.
THIS IS A HANDY WAY OF TAKING CARE OF THE PROBLEM.

THE VARIABLES A AND A(C) ARE TOTALLY DIFFERENT.

THE REASON WE DON'T READ A(C) IS BECAUSE SOME BASICS GET CONFUSED TRYING IT.

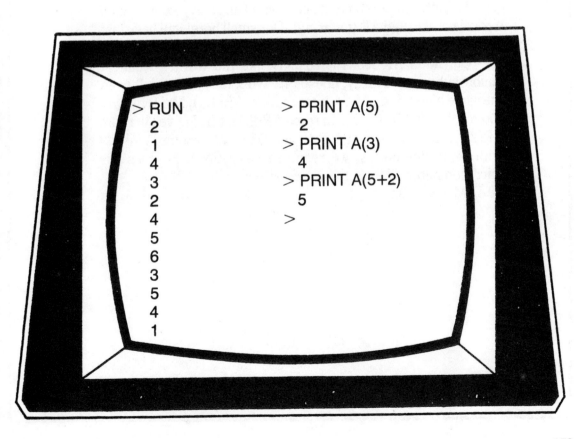

Now that you have seen an example of a single subscripted array, let's look at an example of the world's smallest double subscripted array.

Sure doesn't look like much to get excited about, does it? But wait. Like so many good magic tricks, you can be deceived by the seeming simplicity of an array.

An array is built and governed by laws controlling two factors—rows and columns. Law number one is that rows go from left to right. Law number two is that columns go top to bottom.

To better understand the concept of an array, we will build a small hotel called AR (for array). Our small hotel will have just four rooms.

Our hotel AR looks amazingly like the world's smallest double subscripted array, doesn't it? Well, they were built from the same blue prints. Mr. A lives in room AR(1,1), Mr. B lives in room AR(1,2). Mr. C lives in room AR(2,1). Mr. D lives in room AR(2,2). How did we get A,B,C, and D in those rooms. Why, as with most nice hotels, we require reservations. So does our microcomputer. Here's the reservation:
10 DIM AR(2,2)

WORLD'S SMALLEST DOUBLE
SUBSCRIPTED ARRAY

HOTEL AR

The DIM power simply tells the microcomputer to save space in memory for our array. We give the computer the largest room number we will need, and BASIC knows enough to create the smaller room numbers automatically. When we DIM(2,2) we create all of the room numbers. The room numbers are actually the double subscripts we talked about earlier. Now, since we made reservations, we can put the people in their rooms.

```
20 LET AR(1,1)=A
30 LET AR(1,2)=B
40 LET AR(2,1)=C
50 LET AR(2,2)=D
```

There. Our hotel is full. But, our guests are awfully quiet because they have no personalities. As a matter of fact, they have no values. We will dress them up with important dates.

```
15 A=1066:B=1492:C=1918:D=1929
```

Now, if someone rushes up and asks you when was the battle of Hastings, you can order your microcomputer to PRINT AR(1,1) and get the answer. AR(1,2) would do the same thing for when Columbus discovered America, AR(2,1) would tell you when World War I ended, and AR (2,2) would tell you when the stock market crashed. So, even the world's smallest double subscripted array can be useful.

You really can't do a whole lot with an array this small, so the next logical step is to build a bigger array that would serve a useful purpose. Here are some examples. DIM AR(2,2). DIM AR(4,4). DIM AR(8,8). The first array could hold four values, the second array could hold sixteen values, and the third array could hold sixty-four values. The first array would have two rows and two columns, the second arrays would have four rows and four columns, and the third array would have eight rows and eight columns. The only limit on the size of an array is the amount of RAM memory available to manage the array.

As we illustrated earlier, we can fill an array with a series of LET powers, such as LET AR(1,1)=A. This is tiresome and does not use the power in a microcomputer to the fullest extent. We will use FOR/NEXT loops to build our array. (If you have forgotten how nested FOR/NEXT loops work, be certain to review the FOR/NEXT section in Group 4.)

10 DIM AR(2,2)	Reserves the boxes
20 FOR R=1 TO 2	Starts loop 1
30 FOR C=1 TO 2	Starts loop 2
40 READ A	Reads the data
50 LET AR(R,C)=A	Puts data into array
60 NEXT C,R	Ends both loops
70 DATA 1066, 1492, 1918, 1929	The data

.
.
.

Using data from the array doesn't erase it. You can change it by writing something new to a particular subscript. You cannot change the subscripts, however. Once an array is dimensioned (DIM) it must stay that size throughout the program.

The next program shows a string array.

```
 10 DIM A$(2,3)
 20 LET A$(1,1)="CAT  "
 30 LET A$(1,2)="DOG  "
 40 LET A$(1,3)="EATING "
 50 LET A$(2,1)="THE "
 60 LET A$(2,2)="IS "
 70 LET A$(2,3)="EECCHH!! "
 80 PRINT A$(2,1)+A$(1,2)+A$(2,2);
 90 PRINT A$(1,3)+A$(2,1)+A$(1,1);
100 PRINT A$(2,3)
110 END
```

THIS SHOWS THAT EACH SUBSCRIPTED
VARIABLE IS INDEPENDENT FROM THE
OTHERS IN THE ARRAY. YOU MAY HAVE
TO USE & INSTEAD OF + ON YOUR COMPUTER.

```
> RUN
 THE DOG IS EATING THE CAT EECCHH!!
>
```

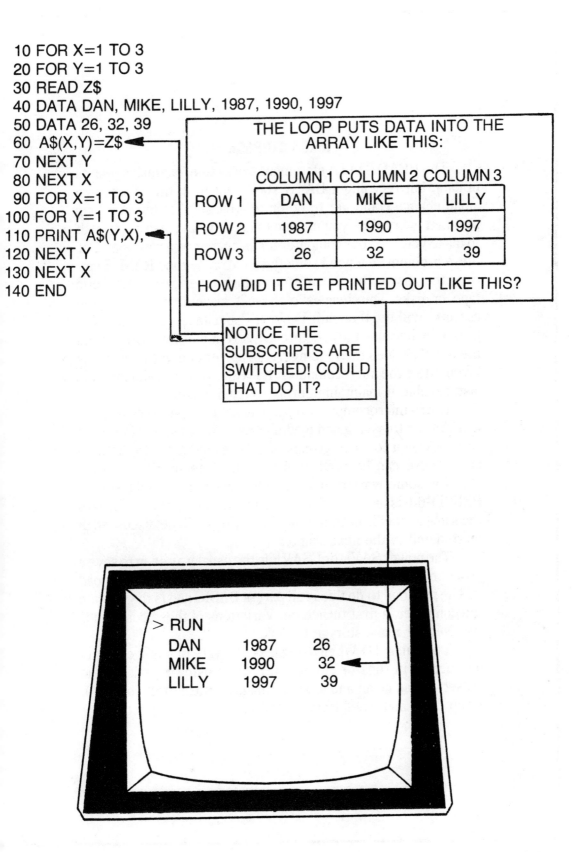

```
10 FOR X=1 TO 3
20 FOR Y=1 TO 3
30 READ Z$
40 DATA DAN, MIKE, LILLY, 1987, 1990, 1997
50 DATA 26, 32, 39
60  A$(X,Y)=Z$
70 NEXT Y
80 NEXT X
 90 FOR X=1 TO 3
100 FOR Y=1 TO 3
110 PRINT A$(Y,X),
120 NEXT Y
130 NEXT X
140 END
```

THE LOOP PUTS DATA INTO THE ARRAY LIKE THIS:

	COLUMN 1	COLUMN 2	COLUMN 3
ROW 1	DAN	MIKE	LILLY
ROW 2	1987	1990	1997
ROW 3	26	32	39

HOW DID IT GET PRINTED OUT LIKE THIS?

NOTICE THE SUBSCRIPTS ARE SWITCHED! COULD THAT DO IT?

```
> RUN
DAN      1987      26
MIKE     1990      32
LILLY    1997      39
```

MASS STORAGE

The READ/DATA statement works fine for small amounts of data, but retyping a DATA statement each time there is a small change could get to be quite a hassel. Typing in a long program every time you needed to use it would also be enough to make you use your computer for an anchor on a row boat. For these problems we need something extra, beyond RAM. Typically the answer has been paper punch tape, cards, magnetic tape, or disks. The cheapest of these is magnetic tape. A simple cassette will do, though it is slow. Paper tape and cards were passed by because they require a different unit for writing from the one that does the reading. A cheap version of the disk was invented for the microcomputer. It is called the mini-floppy. It is fast, reliable if maintained properly, and expensive.

Every microcomputer made has some cassette capability. It is limited to saving and loading programs on some, but most will allow you to write groups of data (called files) to the tape also. These can be read back into the computer as needed. Usually some variation of PRINT such as PRINT#-1 or PRINT#6-6 is used to save files, and a variation of INPUT with the same syntax is used to read them. Files will be discussed in more detail in the next chapter.

The power SAVE or CSAVE is the usual way seen to save a program on tape. LOAD, CLOAD, and OLD are used to reload it. The program to do this is all part of BASIC and is there when the computer is first turned on. Variations of these commands are used for mass storage to disk.

Two rules: (1) When using disks beware of static electricity such as in rugs or clothes. (2) When using tape keep the cassette head clean and aligned (manuals rarely tell you this). Keep disks and tapes from electrical coils and magnets.

PRINTERS

Only a few years ago, when the smallest computers available went for $50,000, spending $3,000—5,000 for a printer was not a significant problem. As the price of computers plummeted downward the price of printers didn't. Today, you can have a $2200 printer hooked up to a $400 computer. In fact, I know a man who did!

Printers are a prime example of a consumer item that is priced, not according to what it costs to make, but by what the market will bare. For this reason price and quality have little in common. To determine what quality is in a printer we must know a few terms.

parallel: Method of sending all eight data lines that make up a byte (and therefore a single character) at the same time (extensions of the data and address lines) on back, a parallel printer usually requires little extra hardware.

serial: Method of sending all of the data, one line at a time, over a single wire. Most computers do not have special ports built in, so extra hardware (an interface) is required to use a serial printer.

pin fed : Means that the printer uses the kind of paper with little holes along the edges. This paper is expensive.

tractor: When the paper is held by rubber rollers, so any paper or pre-printed forms can be used.

thermal: When the characters are burned into a specially treated paper. Thermal printers are usually dot matrix.

impact: Means that some part of the printer physically hits the ink ribbon, transferring the ink onto the paper. It could be dot matrix or letter qualilty.

letter quality: When each character is solid, made by a type head, like a typewriter.

dot matrix: When the print head is made up of a block of little pins. Each pin can strike the ribbon, making a small dot. The printer builds the character from these little dots. Some companies claim to have letter quality dot matrix. They don't. A dot matrix printer can print special characters, like graphics, which letter-quality printers can't.

descenders: Parts of some lower case letters that descend below the line. Some printers can't print these, so the entire character is above the line, which is difficult to read.

buffer: When the computer can send characters much faster than the printer can print them. Some printers have a READY or BUSY line that keeps the computer from sending data until the printer is ready. Others have their own buffer or memory. When this is full the computer waits until the whole buffer is printed before sending another buffer full. Printers with buffers are faster.

Your own needs will dictate, more than anything, what is a good deal for you. A parallel printer at $600 might be a better buy than a serial one at $399 by the time you add in the price of a serial interface. If you must be able to print on your own business form, then no price is a deal on a pin fed printer. Most publishers will accept manuscripts on a dot matrix, but John Q. Public will not respond well to an offer made by the same non-descender, dotty little printer. To set type for a book nothing short of a letter-quality, proportional-spacing printer will do. If you need carbon copies the printer must be impact.

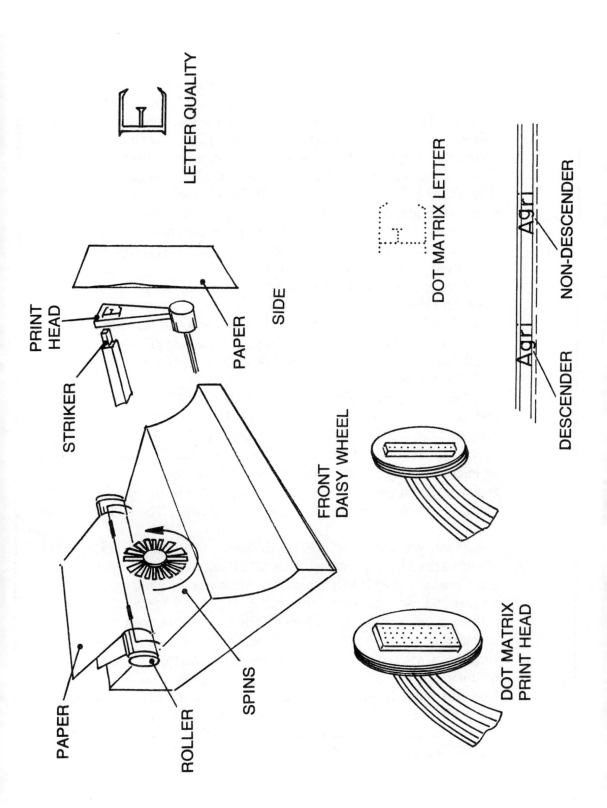

LETTER QUALITY

PRINT HEAD

STRIKER

PAPER

SIDE

PAPER

ROLLER

SPINS

FRONT
DAISY WHEEL

DOT MATRIX
PRINT HEAD

DOT MATRIX LETTER

Agri

Agri

DESCENDER

NON-DESCENDER

The choice is yours.

Output to a printer is handled in many different ways. For many microcomputers the PRINT power is simply changed to LPRINT. The text is formatted on the paper in the same way it was formatted on the screen when using PRINT. Some have variations of PRINT with the same syntax as was used for cassette output, but with a different numeric argument (PRINT#6-6 for cassette and PRINT#6-2 for printer, for example). Some that require serial printers have options within the command that allow you to specify speed, port number, and other variable factors. There are a few that don't print to printers at all.

Printers have their own ASCII code interpreters inside of them, and this can cause difficulty. As mentioned before, the code is fairly standard for uppercase characters and numbers, but punctuation and lowercase codes vary. So do graphic codes, which many printers can't print. For this reason, if you use CHR$ watch out.

When you were experimenting with CHR$ earlier, you may have noticed that the numbers 1 - 12 did some strange things on the screen. This is because those codes are actually specific instructions to the printer. These are almost universal to microcomputers. Your manual should have the list in an appendix. If you are using a printer that is not sold by the people you bought your computer from, watch out again. The codes could vary.

When you command BASIC to output to the printer, it branches to a block of chip instructions in itself called the *printer driver routine*. Most BASICS have ways that you can ignore that routine and use a different one, either written by yourself or sold with the printer you choose. There are *many* printers around that require you to load a special driver, and most of the time it is worth the effort as this custom driver will allow you to do things with the printer that BASIC will not allow. You should have no trouble if you read the documentation that comes with the printer. Don't let the need for a special driver steer you away from a particular printer, UNLESS THEY REQUIRE YOU TO WRITE IT YOURSELF AND YOU DON'T KNOW HOW!

Chapter 7

Sorting Out Your Future

As in every other field of human endeavor, computerists tend to specialize. The two rough categories are hardware and software. Designing hardware takes a certain genius and most people don't qualify. But all the hardware in the world isn't good for much more than scrap without software. Fortunately writing software is something almost anyone can do. All you need to understand is how to define your problem and then translate the steps into a high level language like BASIC. This is called application programming, and there are thousands of unfilled positions in this area. Here is an example of the kind of problem an applications programmer solves every day.

Let's say you are the person responsible for a computer-controlled mailing list available for customers in the business world. Your list contains fifty thousand names and addresses from all fifty states. The first customer orders your mailing list for distribution in all fifty states and you can run the program instantly for them. The second customer only wants to mail to people who live on the Atlantic seaboard. The third customer wants to mail only to customers west of the Mississippi River. The fourth customer only wants to mail to people in Dallas, Texas. As you can see, someone who sets up your computerized mailing list would have to have planned way ahead to be able to meet the demands of customers two, three, and four.

You say this sounds like a pretty small fire? Right! But someone has to do it and a million other tasks just like it everyday. And someone is paying them good money too!

SORTS

Another software area deals not with programs used for a specific purpose, but with programs for general purposes. These are harder to write, but once written are used over and over as a part of many different application programs. These are called utility programs. Sorts are a type of utility and, lest the sample misleads you into believing they are simple, whole volumes have been written about just one kind of sort.

To do this kind of programming requires a good knowledge of what the applications programmer needs in a variety of situations. This way you can write one utility that will work for all of them. A utility programmer spends much more time on a single program than an applications programmer. For instance, it may take a utility programmer a year to write four routines; a search, a sort, a general disk input, and a general printer output. Using these, an applications programmer could solve our mailing list problem in a couple of weeks. All he or she would have to do is define the format of the data and choose which options the customer will be offered. The same routines could then be used in the next program.

Even if you are not going to use a utility over again, this is a good way to break down your program. Then write and test each utility separately. In the end your finished program will be much more flexible and probably have fewer errors.

```
 10 DIM A$(30)
 20 PRINT "HOW MANY WORDS";
 30 INPUT N
 40 FOR K=1 TO N
 50 INPUT A$(K)
 60 NEXT K
 70 PRINT TAB(10)"ALPHABETIZING"
 80 FOR K=1 TO N-1
 90 IF A$(K+1)> = A$(K) THEN GOTO 140
100 B$=A$(K+1)
110 A$(K+1)=A$(K)
120 A$(K)=B$
130 GOTO 80
140 NEXT K
150 FOR K=1 TO N
160 PRINT A$(K)
170 NEXT K
```

THIS VALUE CAN BE BROUGHT INTO THE ROUTINE FROM ELSEWHERE, WHEN USED AS A UTILITY.

THIS LOOP JUST INPUTS THE DATA. IT WOULD ALREADY BE IN AN ARRAY WHEN USING THIS AS A UTILITY.

THIS JUMP STARTS THE ROUTINE OVER. IT INSURES THAT IT WON'T QUIT UNTIL EVERYTHING IS SORTED.

THIS PART IS JUST A PRINTOUT. IT IS NOT NEEDED WHEN USING ROUTINE AS A UTILITY.

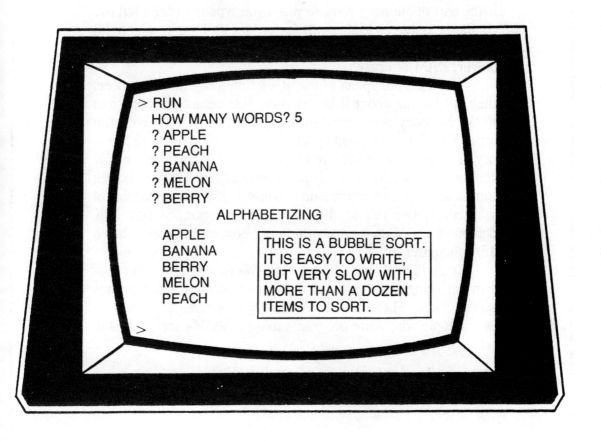

```
> RUN
HOW MANY WORDS? 5
? APPLE
? PEACH
? BANANA
? MELON
? BERRY
        ALPHABETIZING

APPLE
BANANA
BERRY
MELON
PEACH

>
```

THIS IS A BUBBLE SORT. IT IS EASY TO WRITE, BUT VERY SLOW WITH MORE THAN A DOZEN ITEMS TO SORT.

ROMS

Even for the beginner a little taste of hardware is in order. You are already aware of the fact that BASIC is itself just a program being run by the computer that lets it understand what you have written in BASIC text. That program resides in ROM. ROM stands for Read Only Memory.

RAM stands for Random Access Memory. While ROM and RAM are both types of memory, they have almost nothing in common. ROM always remembers whatever was put in it at the factory, such as a language. In small computers, RAM forgets everything it knows each time the computer is turned off. RAM is the part of memory you use when you type in orders, but the computer only remembers those orders as long as electrical power is going into computer memory. If the computer loses power, RAM is erased.

When people speak of the size of memory in a computer, they are talking about RAM because you cannot put orders in ROM. Memory is referred to in increments of 1024, with the letter K used to represent approximately 1000. The more memory a computer has, the more work a computer can do. So, a 16K computer would mean a computer able to store about sixteen thousand pieces of information, while a 32K computer could store thirty-two thousand pieces of information. Since a 32K computer would do more work, it will cost more money than a 16K computer.

You will probably never add ROMs to your computer, but there are languages that will allow you to directly use routines stored there. These are the assembly languages.

People who write programs to go in ROMs are well paid.

COMPILERS AND INTERPRETERS

A computer can respond to humans in dozens of languages, such as Fortran, Cobol, and BASIC. Compilers and interpreters are the software that tell a computer what language to speak. For each language you wish to use in a computer, you must either have it in ROM, or feed the compiler or interpreter into RAM for that language.

Large computers with great memory capability can use many languages at the same time, but again, someone at some time must put in a compiler or interpreter for each language.

Not every compiler or interpreter for each language is the same size. As an example, a large company will sell a compiler or interpreter for five thousand dollars. A small computer company will offer to sell the same language in a compiler or interpreter for sixty-nine dollars. Obviously, there must be a difference, and there is. Almost every computer language has gone through a series of changes to make the language fit into smaller and smaller computers. The problem is, by the time the langauge is condensed to take up less memory, many of the powers in the language are lost. The name of the language remains, but not all of the powers.

There is one major difference between compilers and interpreters. An interpreter stays in memory with the text and executes the text as it decodes it. It must decode it everytime it runs the program. A compiler decodes the text first, and then erases itself from memory. The decoded program can be executed directly by the computer without having to be decoded anymore. This means a compiled program runs much faster and can be much longer because nothing else is sharing memory space with it.

The BASIC in ROM in your computer is an interpreter.

WHAT'S NEXT?

The United States will become the most powerful computer force on earth. This will not require any great effort on the part of anyone. This situation will evolve naturally for five reasons.

The first reason is the English language. With twenty-six letters, this language is easily controlled by a simple keyboard and the language uses up little memory. For many other languages, both these points will prove difficult. The language is known around the world because of commerce. The language is the most popular second language in the world. So, computer programs written in English are most likely to be useful to others. Usefulness is the only consideration to use computer time. English will dominate.

The second reason is the lack of censorship in this country. Almost any computer can be attached to a printer. Once attached, the computer has the potential to be used as a publishing house. In parts of the world, that is a power the government will not allow in the hands of the public. In those countries, simple copy machines are kept under strict supervision. Since a computer is a much more powerful device, supervision will be greater. In those countries, computers will be restricted to military, scientific, and business areas, with all programs carefully regulated. As a result, progress with computers will be seriously hampered.

The third reason is the open structure of education in the United States. In spite of the many faults in public education, one of the great assets is the relative freedom allowed to the individual teacher in classroom activities. Whether through math departments, business departments, or English departments, thousands of computers will enter classrooms across the country. The entry will start, or has started, in colleges and universities, but the real invasion will be at the junior high and high school level. This invasion should have far-reaching effects.

Without going into too much speculation, the importance of computers in education is the introduction of the finest minds in our schools to the boundless potential of computers at an earlier and earlier age. If we have been surprised at computer-wrought changes over the past five years, we may be astonished by computer-wrought changes in the future.

The fourth reason is our all-around technology. Computers by themselves are not all that much, but when harnassed to other equipment, their power multiplies. CAD (Computer Assisted Design) and CAM (Computer Assisted Manufacturing) are general terms to identify two possible avenues for future computer applications in the business world. But, you cannot use a computer to design better cars if you do not manufacture cars. (Well, you could, but it would look silly.) Computers will join with satellites to revolutionize communications, entertainment, and home life—but you must have satellites.

The fifth reason, a negative one, is security. The first computer run and computer-secured homes will be something of a sales gimmick. But, the computer controlled home is as certain as anything can be that does not yet exist.

You may be wondering if the limited knowledge you now have about computers can some day help you get a job working with computers. An obvious answer is: it can't hurt. But, let's take a few minutes to consider some of the problems you will face.

First, microcomputers are still regarded as "toys" by a majority of the people in business and industry. You could point out to them that one of the space shuttle systems depends on a popular microcomputer that performed perfectly on the initial launch but don't expect them to be impressed.

Second, schools at all levels are having a difficult time trying to budget hardware to give realistic training on computers. This lack of trained people will restrict computer growth, even in companies desperately needing to convert to computer applications.

Third, people working in personnel offices do not understand how experience on some hardware can be transferred to other hardware. Indeed, few people in the computer industry have this knowledge, so you can hardly expect the personnel departments to come up with it. This leads to job descriptions or job openings with experience required on specific pieces of hardware. While some hardware applications are unique, the vast majority of computer applications are almost identical, but you cannot depend on personnel people to know this.

Fourth, there is a natural desire of those people already working with computers not to recognize skills learned on computers different from the computer they learned on. In other words, most of the people who now have computer jobs learned their skill on big main frame computers. Naturally, they have not spent much time working microcomputers, so they will not be aware of how fast small computers have developed.

Don't let these problems discourage you. If you choose to seek a job working with computers, you will succeed. This is assured because the shortage of skilled people in just one area, computer programming, is estimated by the government to stand at one million openings right now. This shortage is also estimated to be growing by one hundred thousand unfilled openings per year.

You can fill one of these openings if you will follow some simple advice.

You must build a portfolio, exactly as an actor or model does. In this portfolio you will put all your experience. Include a fairly accurate log of how many hours you have had with "hands-on" experience. Do not apologize if this experience is limited to microcomputers. Anyone who is not intelligent enough to realize the BASIC language learned on a microcomputer is just as valid as the BASIC language learned on an IBM 360 is not someone you should be working for anyway. (After you finish this book, much of what you will learn about computers will come from fellow workers or supervisors, so choose both carefully.)

Much more important than anything else in your portfolio is the collection of programs you will include. These programs will include a LIST and RUN of every program you pick from your personal efforts as your best, any program you have written with someone else, and any program you have studied and understand. Don't depend on a computer being available to show these off. Get printed copies, even if you have to rent a printer. Hard copy is much better than tapes or disks to people, particularly people who may not know computers.

Before going to any job interview, whenever possible, do research. Find out anything you can about any equipment the company uses. Get advertising about that computer from the company or the sales people who sell it. Study this before you go to the interview.

If you are mailing in an interview rather than going to an interview, include in the application sample copies of your own programs and be certain each one carries your copyright line at the top.

During an interview, present your portfolio and politely offer to explain any program you included. Point out that you did not write all of them, but explain that you included them to show what your areas of interest are in computers. (Obviously, be certain you know each program and you can explain them clearly.) Before you offer to explain the programs, find out how much computer experience the person doing the interview has. Do not take the chance of overload and BURNOUT during an interview.

There is a simple rule to follow when you attempt to enter employment as a computer person. Tie your computer skills to knowledge or skills you already have, or tie your computer skills to an area of great interest and desire. Business applications are an old story. Consider writing a new story.

If you are a first string football player, but you are not going to get into professional ball because of your size, seek a coaching job and use a computer to help you recruit or draft.

If you want to go to Hollywood, read up on the new process that uses computers to reduce the cost of animation, and then send an application to the movie studios that specialize in animation.

If you want to be a secret agent, read up on computer use to decode or scramble messages, and then send an application to the government agencies involved in secret communications.

If you want to join a circus, read up on transportation costs, truck versus rail statistics, and then send in your application.

There are no limits. Do what you want to do. You will have to work hard to succeed in jobs on computers just like anything else in life, but if you pick the right field, the field where you most want to work, you will succeed.

When the day comes, good luck.

RANDOM PRINTS—OR "POOR CHARLEY'S ALMANAC"

Never hook up another piece of equipment (like disks or printers) to your computer while it is turned on. You can fry the chips but you can't eat them.

* * * * *

Q. Do I need a lot of math to work with computers?

A. *You only need to be able to read and write the English language.*

* * * * *

The BASIC language is a little like gasoline. Everyone claims theirs is different because they have added something to it. This makes no difference. There is a small BASIC and a big BASIC. The big BASIC has more orders the computer will obey. Know which one you have and forget the rest.

* * * * *

Q. Which computer is best for business uses?

A. *Any, to start.*

Don't write long programs. Expand short ones that work.

* * * * *

Q. Am I too old to work with computers?

A. *Only if you are dead.*

* * * * *

The smallest, cheapest printer on the market is better than not having a printer.

* * * * *

Q. What can a computer do for me?

A. *Anything you are capable of telling it to do.*

In all probability more deliberate lies have been told about computer hardware than any other human experience with the possible exception of weight loss.

* * * * *

Q. What size computer should I buy?
A. *The biggest one you can afford.*

* * * * *

In the future, language skills will be more important than math skills for computer programming.

* * * * *

Q. Should parents allow their children to play with computers at school?
A. *Only if they anticipate graduation.*

Always reserve line numbers 1 through 9 for emergencies in a program. An emergency is when you reach line number 5000 in a program and you discover you left out one hundred variables needed for your program to RUN.

* * * * *

Q. Will computers take over the world?

A. *If there is one.*

* * * * *

The only limitations in using a small computer are in the brain of the person at the Keyboard.

* * * * *

Q. Why is it that every time I ask someone for advice about computers, I get a different answer?

A. *There is more than one computer.*

Anyone who knows a foreign language should consider using a computer to teach that language to others, or consider using a computer to teach English to those who know that language.

* * * * *

Q. My partner says computers will be cheaper next year. Is that true?
A. *Certainly, but without a computer, will your business be here next year?*

* * * * *

Put a correct copyright on every program you store permanently. These days, programs are stolen faster than hubcaps.

* * * * *

Q. How smart are computers?
A. *A binary computer can tell the difference between the symbols 1 and 0. That's it.*

Q. Is it true that computers can ruin the minds of young people?
A. *Only if the young people beat their heads on them.*

* * * * *

In the very near future, computers will have a much greater impact on correspondence and communications than on accounting or bookkeeping.

* * * * *

Q. Should I buy a computer to go with my furniture or with my rug?
A. *Buy one to go with your wallet.*

* * * * *

And if you didn't like this book, well, here is my last piece of advice:

Don't buy any computer books by mail unless you have looked at a copy personally. Too many books are being sold by too many publishers too fast, and the quality of writing in the books is fading fast.

Index

What To Do When You Get Your Hands On A Microcomputer

by Charles P. Holtzman

Here's a fun-to-read *and* informative introduction to computer programming that's suitable for every age group! Written in a lively, easy-to-follow format, it makes it easy to grasp fundamental programming concepts and immediately gives the reader confidence and a sense of achievement. It explains BASIC language and shows how it can be used on any small computer, using cartoon-like drawings to reinforce the most important points.

It starts at square one by explaining that software is the key to getting a computer to live up to its capabilities. You'll be introduced to the basic computer components: crt, keyboard, line numbers, and memory—each one explained in easy-to-understand layman's language. Then you'll learn four sets of BASIC words needed to program your machine—each set arranged in order of complexity and power. First, you'll meet LET, PRINT, END, and RUN. CLS, LIST, NEW, DELETE, and ERROR come next. Then it's on to TAB, MATH POWERS, INPUT, GOTO, IF ...THEN, and RANDOM... and finally you'll cover FOR/NEXT and READ/DATA.

From here, you'll progress to learning more about variables, strings, arrays, and tables; sorts, printer routines, tape saving and loading, and words to control these are thoroughly covered.

Also included: more advanced info on compilers, ROMs, some tips on planning a career in computing, and tongue-in-cheek advice on how to get the most from your computer, your programs, and your programming efforts.

So if you're a novice computerist, or have some youngsters who've been urging you to let *them* learn how to use your machine, this book is one that can make it easy and fun to learn the art of computer programming!

TAB TAB BOOKS Inc.

Blue Ridge Summit, Pa. 17214

Prices higher in Canada

ISBN 0-8306-1397-8